TV FIREFIGHTERS

By

Richard C. Yokley

Black Forest Press
San Diego, California
February, 2003
First Edition

Relive the history of the world's love affair with firefighters by visiting TV programs that have entertained audiences for almost fifty years.

TV FIREFIGHTERS

By

Richard C. Yokley

Published in the United States of America
By
Black Forest Press
P.O. Box 6342
Chula Vista, CA 91909-6342
1-800-451-9404

Disclaimer

This document is an original work of the author. It may include reference to information commonly known or freely available to the general public. Any resemblance to other published information is purely coincidental. The author has in no way attempted to use material not of his own origination without identifying the source. Black Forest Press disclaims any association with or responsibility for the ideas, opinions or facts as expressed by the author of this book. No dialogue is totally accurate or precise. While the book is as accurate as the author can make it, there may be errors, omissions, or inaccuracies.

Permission to use the photos contained herein from many of the photographers, networks, and production companies has been obtained where known and possible. It is not the intent to use any photo against the wishes of its legal owner. All photos are identified as to network, film studio, or photographer.

All the information contained within these pages is provided for educational, entertainment, and information purposes only, and no infringement is intended! Nothing contained herein shall create any liabilities whatsoever. I have no connection with any of the shows presented here. Like you, I am a fan, providing information I hope other fans will find useful.

No part of this book including photos may be used or reproduced in any manner whatsoever without prior written permission from the author, except by a reviewer who may quote brief passages in a review.

Richard C. Yokley has asserted the moral right to be identified as the author of this work.

Printed in the United States of America
Library of Congress
Cataloging-in-Publication

ISBN: 1-58275-081-5
Copyright February, 2003 Richard C. Yokley

ALL RIGHTS RESERVED

> *"A funny thing about firemen – night or day – they're always firemen!"*
> — *Ronald, the arsonist, in Backdraft*

DEDICATION

To my wife Jean and our children, Rick and Karin. For all those missed holidays, birthdays, and anniversaries I spent at the firehouse.

The events of September 11, 2001 have touched us all. A good friend commented, "I really did not know until now (Sept. 11) what all you guys did." Some TV programs, including documentaries, written long before the tragedy that include FDNY writers, extras, advisors, and firefighters are no longer with us.

As Firefighters, Police Officers, EMT's, or Paramedics we always try to do our best by rushing in where others fear to tread, while others are rushing out - to save what we can - do our job, and then some. Not always successful, but we try, and occasionally we lose some of our own in the process. For all those who have lost their lives, to their families, and to those who have become so seriously injured they are unable to return to the job they love – this book is dedicated to you!

ACKNOWLEDGMENTS

This book would not have been possible without the continued support of Erika Bartlett and Rozane Sutherland – whose *Emergency!* website and friendship has allowed me to reach more people around the world than I ever thought possible.

The information contained herein is culled from personally conducted interviews with technical advisors, consultants, writers, producers, fans, actors, researchers, filmographers, authors, and many others, as well as listings, reviews, and articles from entertainment industry publications. All of which are listed throughout and at the end of this book. Please forgive me if I have omitted anyone.

TABLE OF CONTENTS

Introduction		xiii
Chapter 1	**THE BEGINNING**	1
	Alarm (1954)	
	Alarm (1956)	
	Code 3	
	Whirlybirds	
	Chicago 2-1-2	
	Rescue 8	
	Where There's Smokey	
	Lassie	
	The Ballad of Smokey The Bear	
	The Smokey Bear Show	
Chapter 2	**EMERGENCY!**	11
Chapter 3	**THE 1970's**	33
	Lassie's Rescue Rangers	
	Firehouse	
	Emergency+ 4	
	Go	
	Sierra	
	The Rangers	
	905-Wild	
	Pine Canyon Is Burning	
	Code-R	
	240-Robert	
	Chopper One	
	Chopper Squad	
Chapter 4	**THE 1980's**	47
	Code Red	
	Firefighter	
	Rescue 911	

Chapter 5	**THE 1990's**	55
	H.E.L.P.	
	Code 3	
	Philly Heat	
	Firehouse	
	L.A. Firefighters	
	Fire Co. 132	
	Firehouse 421	
	The 119	
	Family Brood	
	St. Michael's Crossing	
	Rescue 77	
	Firehouse One	
	Rescue Heroes	
Chapter 6	**THIRD WATCH**	79
	Third Watch starts and ends its third season on a somber note	
	About the FDNY and 9/11	
Chapter 7	**THE 2000's**	102
	The C-Shift	
	Superfire	
	Romeo Fire	
	Boomtown	
Chapter 8	**NON FIRE-THEMED SERIES WITH FIREFIGHTER CHARACTERS**	111
Chapter 9	**ON THE DRAWING BOARD**	117
	USAR-1	
	Search & Rescue	
Chapter 10	**REALITY TV PROGRAMS**	121
Chapter 11	**DOCUMENTARIES**	131
Chapter 12	**DIARY OF AN ARSONIST**	143
Chapter 13	**9/11-RELATED DOCUMENTARIES**	147

Chapter 14	**INTERNATIONAL TV FIREFIGHTERS**	157
	Australia — Police-Rescue	
	Fire	
	Emergency 000	
	Canada — Forest Rangers	
	In the Line of Duty	
	Caserne 24	
	Fire Station	
	China — Burning Flame	
	Burning Flame II	
	England — Fire Crackers	167
	The Firefighters	
	London's Burning	
	Casualty	
	Boon	
	999	
	Firefighters	
	Reality TV	
	Finland — Pelastajat	182
	112 Auttajat	
	France — SOS 18	
	Germany — Feuerwache 09	
	Spritzen-Karli, Der	
	Alarm Code 112	
	Hungary — Trombi és a Tüzmanó	
	Ireland — Firewatch / D-Watch (1999)	185
	Firewatch (2002)	
	Japan — Faiyâman	
	Kynkyu Hashin Saver Kids	
	Mexico — Operacion Rescate	
	Singapore — Code Red	
	995	
	Sweden — Nile City 105.6	
	Switzerland — Alarm	
	Wales — Fireman Sam	

Chapter 15	**CROSSOVER COLLECTABLES**	189
Chapter 16	**5 - 5 - 5 - 5**	193
Chapter 17	**SPECIAL EFFECTS**	197
Chapter 18	**INTERESTING TIDBITS**	201

    Crossword puzzles
    Firehouses on TV
    LA City Station 27 on Television
    Other Los Angeles fire stations on TV
    It's the Law
    Fireman in other languages
    Emergency call numbers around the world

Chapter 19	**TV PROGRAMS ON THE WEB**	217
Chapter 20	**FIREHOUSE RECIPES**	223
Acknowledgements		251
Bibliography		255
About the Author		259

INTRODUCTION

Believe it or not, there have been close to eighty TV movies and series programs about firefighters over the past fifty years; with new shows emerging and pilots being developed almost every season, most of which will never see the light of a TV screen. Discussing primarily series programming I have included pilots, unaired pilots, spin-offs, mini-series, documentaries, and international programs, in order to be as comprehensive as possible. Some US-produced series programs and pilots, although not shown in the US, have aired in other countries. I have also touched on fire related collectibles that have been produced for many of the programs.

The issue of technical accuracy is always a problem; recreating the life of a firefighter isn't a simple task, especially when dozens of pages of the script must be shot in a single day, often out of order. Be it a program about policemen, lawyers, firefighters, or doctors, the writers and producers take liberties, theorizing that the average viewer would not pick up the inaccuracies. The same complaints are always aired, "No smoke in the building," or "That's not the way it's done." Handstand defibrillation, *Towering Infernos*, million gallons of water on the roof, and other similar issues are a technical assistant's nightmare.

Even *Emergency!* had its problems. We know that lawyers don't try the case of the century every day, every police department (PD) unit does not respond to ten robberies per shift, nor firefighters to several major fires daily. As firefighters we don't save every cardiac arrest victim, our hair is not always combed, and contrary to popular belief not all firefighters are good cooks.

The word "fireman" or "firemen" is used interchangeably with "firefighter." The terminology usage of "firefighter" did not come about until the mid to late 1970's. Use of "fireman" in this book is used as referencing to program press releases for the early programs.

Ratings and demographics are what count for the networks, not accuracy, unfortunately at times, even to the point of embarrassment to the profession. The programs have to entertain and remain exciting. However, we need to remember that these shows, even with some scenes based on actual in-field incidents, they are not reality but reality-based. It's entertainment, and it's television, nothing more!

That said...

CHAPTER ONE — THE BEGINNING

The earliest program I have been able to find is titled *Alarm*. Produced in 1954 this thirty-minute episode opens with a discussion between actor Richard Arlen and Fire Chief Keith Klinger of the Los Angeles County Fire Department. The story is about five fires that have broken out in the same neighborhood in the previous ten days. It stars Richard Arlen as Capt. London, Chick Chandler and J. Pat O'Malley as firemen, and Dick Simmons (*Sgt. Preston of the Yukon*) as Police Lt. Larry Jones. Captain London and fireman McCuen join forces with the Arson Squad to find the firebug responsible. This was to be the first of the syndicated *Alarm* series. Directed by Lewis Foster, it was produced with the full cooperation and assistance of the LA County Fire Department by Roland Reed Productions, from an original idea by Fred Kline. Chief Klinger provided technical assistance. The fire station used for filming was LA County Fire Station 8 in West Hollywood, with its equipment of pumper, truck, and Rescue Squad.

In 1956, the second try for the series was produced again titled *Alarm*, but with a different format. Fred Waring hosted, with Chief Edward Montgomery of the Boston Fire Department. This thirty-minute episode featured the Coconut Grove fire on Nov. 28, 1942, as seen through the eyes of an actor, a couple trying to save their ten-year marriage, and a soldier and his girlfriend. This was a fictionalized account of the tragic fire that took the life of cowboy star Buck Jones amongst 490 others. The pilot starred John Hoyt and Herb Vigran. The opening and ending credits utilized the same fire footage of LA County as did the 1954 pilot. Directed by William Claxon, this format was to focus on different fire incidents around the country. Neither series was developed and it is unknown whether either of them aired.

The following two programs, *'CODE 3'* and *'Whirlybirds'* by definition are not firefighting programs, but crime/adventure programs. But they are the first programs known to air to have some aspect of fire and rescue within the series.

CODE 3 from the Hal Roach Studios, for First-Run Syndication airing in 1956/57 with 39 episodes. This is primarily a police drama and a few are mentioned in this book as they do have rescue/firefighting or fire investigating aspects. *CODE 3* starred Richard Travis as Sheriff Barnett of the Los Angeles County Sheriff Department, along with Denver Pyle as Sgt. Murchison, and Fredd Wayne as Lt. Bill Hollis. In one episode, the sheriff's office attempts to solve a series of baffling fires. A section of comic strip found near the scene of a fire gives the sheriff a clue to the mystery. Another episode deals with a rescue by the Sheriff Department of an injured youth trapped in an abandoned oil derrick. This episode featured DeForest Kelly (*Star Trek*). Guest stars in other episodes were, Russell Johnson (*Rescue 8*), Kenneth Toby (*WhirlyBirds*), Stacy Keach, and Lola Albright. Appearing at the end of most episodes is Eugene W. Biscailuz, real-life Sheriff of Los Angeles County. Produced by Hal Roach, Jr., written by Laurence Menkin, (*Dragnet)* and Directed by Paul Landres, (*Adam 12 - Dragnet*).

Whirlybirds, a Desilu Production, Inc. with CBS Films, Inc., for First-Run Syndication as an adventure series airing three seasons during 1957-60 with 111, 30-minute episodes. Starring Kenneth Tobey as Chuck Martin and Craig Hill as Pete ("P.T.") Moore, the show centered on Martin and Pete, owners of 'Whirlybirds, Inc', who flew their helicopter anywhere where they could to be of help to someone in trouble. *Whirlybirds* was filmed in the Van Nuys area of California. Bell Helicopter Corp. supplied the Bell 47J Ranger and Bell 47G helicopters.

Two episodes dealing with rescue and firefighting were Episode 4 *"Fireflight"*. Chuck and P.T. answer a distress call from three mountain climbers who are about to be over run by a raging forest fire. Episode 60, *"Fear"*, three youths, volunteer firefighters from a juvenile detention camp, are forced to retreat to a canyon when the fire they are fighting surrounds them. Chuck and P.T. rescue them and fly them to a first aid station. Executive Producer Mort Briskin. The idea for the series came from the *I Love Lucy* episode "*Bon Voyage,*" that aired on January 16, 1956. *Whirlybirds* is the first of the helicopter based action programs.

Chicago 2-1-2 aired April 30, 1957, on CBS. The pilot featured Frank Lovejoy as Inspector Ed McCook, a Fire Inspector for the Chicago Fire Department. McCook looks for an arsonist who was hired by a property owner to start fires for insurance purposes, as over 17 fires had been started within the previous month. The show introduced 19-year-old Roy Thinnes (*The Invaders*) as the teenaged arsonist. It was produced with the assistance and cooperation of the Chicago Fire Department by Don Sharp and Warren Lewis, and directed by Norman Foster. Ed Downes was the technical consultant. 2-1-2 was the Morse code signature for the main fire alarm office. It is what the firefighters in the field would tap out on the alarm box key or at the station house watch desk to reach the office. The series was not developed.

In 1958, 14 years before *Emergency!* there was another program about two Los Angeles County fire/rescue personnel, **Rescue 8.** The introduction states, "This program is dedicated to rescue teams throughout the US and to the men who risk their lives daily to save others. And now, the stories behind the rescues." Produced with the cooperation of the LA County Fire Department, it aired for two seasons on NBC with seventy-three thirty-minute black and white episodes. The first season produced thirty-nine episodes and immediately went into syndication by Screen Gems Inc. They were headquartered at Fire Station 8 in West Hollywood at 7643 W. Santa Monica Boulevard, home of the "real" Rescue 8. Very little filming took place there, however, with several episodes taking place while they were off duty.

In an era where firefighters were not allowed to take a patient's blood pressure (as they were not allowed to use stethoscopes), and artificial respiration was the "Back Pressure Arm Lift" method, one episode showed rescue firefighter Cameron performing an emergency appendectomy, while a physician gave instructions via telephone.

Lang Jefferies and Jim Davis of
Rescue 8
Screen Gems Photo

Rescue 8 starred Jim Davis, later known as patriarch Jock Ewing of *Dallas,* as Senior Firefighter Wes Cameron. It also starred Lang Jeffries as his partner, firefighter Skip Johnson, with Nancy Rennick as Skip's wife, and Mary K. Cleary as their daughter. These were the only characters that had recurring roles in the program.

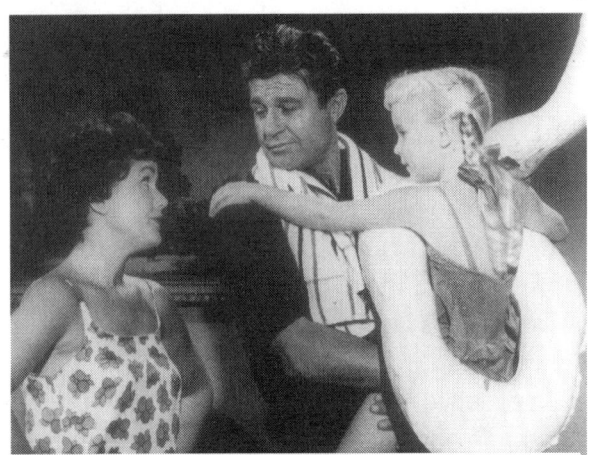

Rescue 8
L-R Nancy Rennick, Jim Davis, Mary K. Cleary
Photo from Mary K. Cleary Collection

TV Firefighters 5

Even though it is stated they lived at 7023 Canyon Blvd. in Los Angeles, according to Cleary, "We had several houses they used on location. The inside is different most of the time, they had a few the same, but most of the time it seems either they forgot how it was set up or they just didn't care then." Even the exterior shots of their home were often changed. Many scenes were filmed at the old KTTV Television Studios in Los Angeles. The young Mary appeared in another rescue series, *Whirlybirds* (a.k.a. *Copter Patrol*).

Joseph Mahaffey was technical consultant, and Ed "Doctor Ed" Elterman, an LA County firefighter, was technical advisor, having worked on the real Rescue 8. Both Davis and Jeffries did ride-a-longs with a Rescue Squad, where they learned how to handle rescue tools such as porta-powers, and SCBA's, administer oxygen, and use the safety harness for Hi-Rise rescues. The vehicle used in the show was a 1948 GMC ½ ton panel truck, and was typical of the vehicles used by LA County during that era; there were twenty-seven rescue units of this type in service at the time.

Jim Davis and Lang Jeffries
Checking the rescue equipment
Screen Gems Photo

Although many of the County's Rescue vehicles were Fords, the real Rescue 8, as well as the vehicle depicted in the program, was a GMC. The rescue units typically responded without the engine, unless requested, which was usually an open cab Crown. LA City and County loved these rigs. First purchased in

1953, they were running first out up through the late 70's. The last one purchased for LA County was in 1976, and Crown went out of business in 1985. LA City ultimately purchased one hundred thirty-eight of these engines. In actuality only one rescue/firefighter manned the rescue, and not until 1968 were they upgraded to two man units. By 1974, all rescue units would be converted to Paramedic Squads. The firefighters received no extra pay for being on the Rescue unit, and promotions were limited. Ambulance transportation in the series was provided by Snyder or Goodhew/LA with a Millers ambulance logo in those old low-boy Cadillacs.

Some notable guest stars were James Best as a rookie firefighter (later to be seen in *Hooper* and *Dukes of Hazzard*), John Carradine, noted for his starring roles in horror movies, Mike Connors (*Mannix*), Jay North (*Dennis the Menace*), and Richard Chamberlain, (*Dr. Kildare, The Thorn Birds*). Also seen were Ellen Corby (The Waltons), Russell Johnson (*Gilligan's Island*), and Warren Oates (Western film character actor and *Blue Thunder*).

Restored 1947 Ford Panel Rescue 11
Owner: Jim Page, who served LA County on R-11
Photo Tom Page Photography, Vista, CA

Prominent photographer Fred Kline's (*Alarm*) apparatus ride-along footage from LA County area was utilized throughout the series. Paul Frees and George Draing created *Rescue 8*. Herbert B. Leonard (*Route 66, Naked City*) produced *Rescue 8* for Screen Gems Inc., a subsidiary of Columbia Pictures, and Wilbert

Productions in association with Cinefilm Inc. To save money in the purchase of film, the production company utilized recycled magnetic film previously used for commercials and other TV programs.

The Assistant Producer and chief writer was Jessie Lasky Jr. Story plots ended within each episode, so there were no continuing storylines. Episodes usually ended with a fire prevention tag in the credits. *Rescue 8* aired in worldwide syndication for several years. It was dubbed into Chinese, German, Spanish, Swedish, and many other languages. It aired most recently on the Nostalgia Television cable channel, (now the GoodLife TV Network).

The Chicago Tribune TV Week of May 9-15, 1959 featured a story and photos of Jim Davis. The April 16-22, 1960 edition of *TV Guide* featured Mary K.Cleary (the daughter). *Rescue 8* also aired in Australia, and in the March 7-13, 1959 New South Wales edition of *TV Times* shows the two stars in a full-page photo. In Australian editions of *TV Week*, the July 23, 1959 edition features Davis and Jeffries on the back cover, and on February 4, 1960, a photo of only Lang Jeffries in fire gear. A rare collectable is a Hi-Ball glass which was distributed by Screen Gems as a promotional item. It featured the names of three TV series that were in production at the time and included *Rescue 8, The Adventures of Rin Tin Tin* (which Mary also appeared in), and *The Man from Blackhawk*.

Where There's Smokey was produced and filmed in 1959 as a pilot for ABC, but did not air until March 3, 1966. It starred comedian Soupy Sales as a klutzy firefighter, Gale Gordon as the Fire Chief who is constantly frustrated by his fireman nephew (Sales), along with Clyde Adler, John Elmen, and Jack Weston. It was written by Sid Dorfman (*Mash, Good Times*) and Rod Amateau, and produced by Dorfman for Desilu Productions. Rod Amateau directed. (This is available as "Soupy Sales Vol.1" on video from Kinevideo.net)

Lassie aired from 1954 through 1974 on CBS. During seasons 10 through 16, (1964 – 1970) Lassie is owned by US Forest Ranger Corey Stuart (Robert Bray). In these episodes we find Lassie performing the usual duties of saving children, adults, and animals from danger. Environmental issues are introduced and several episodes deal with watershed concerns and firefighting. Jack DeMave and Jed Allan are two new USFS Rangers that take over when Stuart is injured in a fire. Two books released during this run were *Forest Ranger Handbook*, by Corey Stuart and Lassie, produced by the USFS in 1967; and *Lassie and the Firefighters* Whitman Tell-A-Tale, 1968 based on the Ranger Corey Stuart character.

One can't forget the firefighting Smokey Bear. At 7:30pm on November 24, 1966, on NBC's General Electric Full Color Fantasy Hour, a sixty-minute Rankin/Bass production of ***The Ballad of Smokey The Bear*** aired. This "animagic" stop-action adventure, narrated by James Cagney as the voice of "Big Bear," told the story of how a timid little bear cub overcame his fears to become the legendary symbol of the United States Forest Service. Produced by Lucerne Media and Videocraft TV, written by Joseph Schrank, with the voice of Barry Pearl as "Smokey." Original music was by Johnny Marks, who also wrote the music and lyrics for the still-popular *Rudolph the Red-Nosed Reindeer*, narrated by Berl Ives.

The Smokey Bear Show, another Rankin/Bass animated production for ABC began airing September 6, 1969 at 8:30am. The half hour series ran through September 12, 1971, with fifty-one original episodes. Long after Smokey was already well established as an American icon, he was given this Saturday morning show. Smokey lived a peaceful life in the forest, along with his neighbors Bessie the pig, Freddie the skunk, Bennie the rabbit, and Gabby the mountain lion.

Together, they would teach each other the ways of the world. But true to his cause, Smokey was always on the alert for fire. Some of his friends weren't always so careful, so he often had to teach them a thing or two. Even when Smokey wasn't talking about fire safety, each episode invariably stressed the importance of preserving the wild. Jackson Weaver, a disc jockey on WMAL in Washington, D.C. became the famous voice of Smokey, the rest of the voice cast were Canadians. The show was titled *El Oso Fumarola* in Mexico.

Over the years, several notable actors have appeared in, or voices heard (James Cagney) in films about Smokey (the) Bear. Other than the two already mentioned, others are classified as Television PSA's, shorts, or films made for schools and range from three minutes in length to over 30 minutes long. Celebrities include Eddie Arnold singing the 'Smokey The Bear' song in the 1950's, and western star Hopalong Cassidy (William Boyd) in a promotion with 'Smokey' the new bear cub in 1953. Also appearing in films were Dennis Weaver in 1971, and Denver Pyle in 1977, who also appeared on a Smokey Bear 50th Anniversary trading card set.

As an aside, the confusion over it being 'Smokey Bear' or 'Smokey The Bear' stems from the original bear cub found in Capitan, New Mexico after a fire in 1950. Smokey artist Rudolph Wendelin explained to me that 'Smokey The Bear' was the "live" bear that lived in the National Zoo in Washington, DC and 'Smokey Bear' is the official U.S. Forestry Service trade mark name for promotions and merchandise.

CHAPTER TWO — EMERGENCY!

Often duplicated – Never equaled

No firefighter/EMS/rescue program before or since had the impact or sustained longevity of *Emergency!* As with Jack Webb's earlier police drama *Adam-12* (1968-1975), which changed the way America perceived its police officers, so did *Emergency!* change the course of firefighter/paramedic programs in this country. Still popular thirty years since first airing, *Emergency!* almost immediately went into syndication in various markets worldwide. It was resurrected for a short time on cable's TV Land (1999-2001), but still can be seen in some US markets, as well as in Canada and Australia, where a whole new generation can watch the exploits of Station 51.

Laugh or scoff if you must, but probably nothing changed the course of emergency medical response in the United States more than this milestone program. Undoubtedly, it was the single most important factor in informing the public about the advancements being made in the Emergency Medical Services (EMS) nationwide. In the fall of 1967, in Miami, Florida, the first "fire department" paramedics hit the streets. "The dramatic series, *Emergency!* was responsible for spreading the word to the four corners of the US, creating the almost instant demand for the services viewed on the family TV set," states Dr. Eugene Nagel. He further states, "I can't think of anything that advanced emergency medicine in this country more than this program did."

LA County's fire department paramedic program began training in September of 1969 at LA County Harbor-UCLA Medical Center. By December 1969, LA County Squad 59, and LA City Rescue Ambulance 53 went into service as the County's first ALS units with nurse ride-a-longs (as noted in the pilot episode of

Emergency!). It wasn't until July 1970, with the signing of the Wedworth-Townsend Paramedic Act by California Governor Ronald Reagan that paramedics were allowed to run calls without the nurses.

By 1971, the LA County Fire Department had three paramedic squads in service: Squad 36 at Station 36 in Carson (just down the street from Station 127, which later became TV's Station 51), Squad 59 based at LA County Harbor-UCLA Medical Center, and Squad 18 in Lennox. All this while Congress was passing legislation to standardize EMS practices nationwide.

The "direct spark for the series" actually began sometime in 1970, when Sid Sheinberg, President of MCA/Universal TV, felt that a "variant of the action-packed realism" in *The Hellfighters*, a 1968 Universal Pictures movie about oil firefighters starring John Wayne, would be just the thing for early evening television. Sheinberg approached television producer Jack Webb (*Dragnet, Adam-12*) with this idea, and asked him to consider developing a series with Universal about a firefighter rescue team. Jack Webb sent Robert A. Cinader, an Executive Producer for Webb's production company, to research the concept of a series about "rescue." Cinader contacted Dick Friend, LA County Fire Department's Public Information Officer (PIO), and was referred to Captain Jim Page at Station 7 in West Hollywood.

On May 11th 1971, Cinader spent several hours at the fire station. Despite Page's efforts to interest Webb and Cinader in the new paramedic program, they were unenthused but hired him to research possible stories for a TV series about "physical rescue." Shortly thereafter, Jim Page was promoted to Battalion Chief, and he invited Bob Cinader to ride along with him and his driver, Dale Cauble, on medical emergencies involving the new paramedics. After Cinader saw the paramedics in action he was convinced that a show featuring paramedics would make for good television. The rest, as they say, is history.

On November 22nd, 1971, filming began for the two-hour *Emergency!* movie (pilot) which took twenty-two shooting days. Ironically, shooting began at LA County's Station 8, its fourth appearance in a series – and not its last – but this time as Station 10. It is here that firefighter Gage was assigned to the Rescue Squad. A recently graduated paramedic, Roy DeSoto, was holding interviews for prospective paramedics at Station 10 for the next class, and was trying to convince Gage to become a paramedic even though they were unable to practice at that time.

Jack Webb (standing) with Randy Mantooth (passenger) and unidentified driver in a promo from the EMERGENCY! pilot. This is the "real" Rescue 8 Dodge with the "10" decal.
Mark VII Production Universal Photo

Time line in the movie: late 1969 then ahead to mid 1970 when they were able to respond without nurses in attendance. *Emergency!* was produced and directed by Jack Webb (his only directorial role for the series, other than one proposed spin-off) for Mark VII Productions and Universal Television, and debuted January 15,

1972, on NBC. Thirteen one-hour episodes were ordered up by NBC to start the mid-season schedule. The one-hour episodes were filmed on a six-day shooting schedule. Rounding out the rest of Station 51's crew were Tim Donnelly as Firefighter Chet Kelly, always the jokester, Firefighter Marco López, the cook of the station, and real LA County Firefighters Engineer Mike Stoker, and Captain Dick Hammer.

Chief Page, while serving as the department's technical consultant to the series, reviewed the dailies and often made recommendations for editing, to assure accuracy and to protect the Department's image. Dale Cauble, one of LA County Fire Department's first paramedics, was the technical advisor for the pilot. Like the earlier *Rescue 8*, the principal characters would be two firefighters, but in this case newly trained paramedics. Randolph Mantooth and Kevin Tighe, earning only $750.00 per episode initially, would forever become known as "Johnny" and "Roy." By the spring of 1974, they were both asking for $7,500.00 an episode. Webb offered a $40,000 bonus if they would see out their seven-year contract at their cur-

Kevin Tighe as
Roy DeSoto
and
Randolph Mantooth
as Johnny Gage
Universal
Television/NBC
Photo

rent salary. They turned that down, and ultimately settled for $4,500.00 per episode. Both even directed a few episodes and Kevin wrote one episode in the last season.

Produced with the full cooperation of the LA County Fire Department, the County Department of Hospitals, the LA County Board of Supervisors, and the Department of Health Services, *Emergency!* ran through September 1977 with 124 one-hour episodes, and always remained in the 28-33 range in overall ratings, airing against tough competition such as *All In The Family*. The hour-long programs cost as little as $185,000 per episode (in 1972 dollars). Six, two-hour, made-for-TV movies aired through 1979, only two of which were filmed in the Los Angeles area of Compton (*Survival on Charter 220*), and Wrightwood (*Steel Inferno*). One filmed in Seattle and two in San Francisco, were made as possible pilots for a future series based on EMS in different cities. The movies failed to live up to the series standard and the proposed series was never developed. A retrospective of past rescues via flashbacks as the two are promoted to Captain, was the last movie filmed, titled *Emergency!'s Greatest Rescues*. Only Kevin and Randy of the crew of 'A' Shift's Station 51 appeared in the movies due to their seven-year contract with the studio.

Emergency! not only entertained audiences but also educated them. According to co-producer Hannah Shearer, Cinader's theory was to teach through entertainment, without the audience knowing they were being educated. By 1976 *Emergency!* was being aired in forty-one countries worldwide, and was named one of TV's Top Ten Shows. Producer Robert Cinader received several awards for his contribution to emergency health services. He was appointed to the LA County EMS Commission in 1975 and served until his death in 1982.

Julie London was nominated for a Golden Globe Award in 1974, for Best TV actress in a Drama Series, for her work in

Emergency! But more important than the awards, both media and personal, was the number of lives saved by the awareness of the EMS system, and how to activate it. *Emergency!* was praised by US Senator Alan Cranston (D-California) for educating the public about the value of real-life paramedic programs. President Richard Nixon himself admitted to watching the show, which resulted in numerous changes in the federal government's role in fire safety, one of which was smoke detectors.

"The wonderful thing about our show," said Kevin Tighe in 1974, "Is that lives have been saved because of it. Paramedic programs have been set up all around the country as a result of our program (*Emergency!*). They are not all necessarily associated with fire departments; some are voluntary. Los Angeles County gets requests from all over asking how to set up paramedic programs. Its just great," stated Kevin. By series end, the LA County Fire Department had thirty-one paramedic squads and four paramedic engines in service. Today, the Department has fifty-five paramedic squads, nine paramedic assessment engines, four paramedic engines, four paramedic squad boats, three air squads, and two EMT-D Lifeguard rescue units stationed on Catalina Island, twenty miles off the California coast.

There were three Captains that served on "A" Shift at Station 51. Dick Hammer as Captain Hammer in Episodes 1.1 through 1.10; John Smith credited as Capt. Hammer in Episode 1.11, *Hang Up* and Episode 1.12, *Crash*. John Smith's real name was Robert "Dutch" Van Orden, and the name "Van Orden" is on his turnout coat, not "Hammer." Michael Norell as Captain Stanley, who joined the cast in season two did ride-alongs in preparation for his role with LA County Fire Captain Morgan Peterson at Station 95. Norell would later write several episodes.

There were two canine mascots throughout the series. In seasons two through five "Boot," a Benji-looking dog inhabited the station, and in season six a Bassett Hound named "Henry". "Don't you call it Hank!" states Capt. Hank Stanley, became Chet's pride and joy.

Station 51, a fictional station number, was created and filmed at Los Angeles (LA) County Station 127, 2049 East 223rd St. in the City of Carson, located South of LA International Airport off the I-405. Station 127 is not a paramedic station and houses a truck and pumper. Since 1985, it has been known as the Robert A. Cinader Memorial Fire Station. Mr. Cinader had worked with Jack Webb on earlier projects as the producer of *Dragnet* and *Adam-12*. LA County now has a real Station 51, a recently dedicated station on the Universal Studios lot at 3900 North Lankershim Blvd., North Hollywood (Universal City). The Universal tram tour goes in front of the station but be prepared to take your photos quickly as the tram does not stop. Old Station 60 is now unused, but more about Fire Station 60 later.

Among those appearing in the recurring roles of Rampart Hospital's ER staff were Robert Fuller as Dr. Kelly Brackett, and Julie London (Jack Webb's ex-wife) as Nurse Dixie McCall, whose portrayals were based on real people at Harbor General, along with Bobby Troup (Julie's husband) as Dr. Joe Early, and Ron Pinkard as Dr. Morton. Stock footage, aerial shots, and long shots of Rampart Hospital utilized LA County Harbor-UCLA Medical Center at 1000 West Carson St. in Torrance, also known as Harbor General Hospital. This is where many of LA City and County's paramedics actually underwent their training. The ambulance entrance to "Rampart" and hospital interior was built on Universal's lot and still stands today. Long gone, however, is Station 51 interiors, kitchen, apparatus bay, and dorm area sets. Fictional Rampart Hospitals phone number is 555-4667. The name for the hospital, "Rampart," came from Jack Webb's *Dragnet*. Rampart Division was where Jack Webb as Sgt. Joe

Friday worked, and is a real division of the LAPD. Dr. Brackett's office at Rampart Hospital is in room 127.

"For Real" (see name badge) Paramedic Mike Lewis, Technical Advisor on 5 episodes with the hospital cast of *Emergency!* "We were doing more than paramedics are allowed to do today."

The last Squad 51 vehicle used in the show was donated to the County of Los Angeles Fire Museum Association in 1998. This is not the Squad used in the pilot. That unit was in service as Squad 36, a 1969 D-300, one-ton, with adhesive numbers "51" on the doors and rear covering the real Squad numbers. At times the producers 'rented' actual squads from the Fire Department. For the most part there were two Dodge models of squads used in the program, and sharp eyes will note in the stock footage that sometimes there are "new" Dodge shots interspersed with the "old" Dodge in the same episode. There was the "real" squad used in the pilot and stock footage, and a 1974, one-ton, D-30 that was used for the completion of the series and two later *Emergency!* TV movies. In 1972, the Chrysler Corporation provided a chassis for the last "Squad 51"

TV Firefighters

and Universal Studio craftsmen constructed the utility body. (According to the Chrysler Corp. the squad is technically a 1972 vehicle, although it was not licensed until 1974).

1974 Dodge Squad 51
Universal Television

This Squad was actually a vehicle owned by and registered to Universal Studios as a commercial vehicle. The studio transportation department was responsible for getting it from the studio to wherever they would be shooting on location each day. A union studio truck driver would drive it on public streets with an actual commercial plate number of 70 324 H, issued by the California Department of Motor Vehicles (DMV). The prop department would then place the Hollywood prop tax-exempt license plate <E> 999007 on the vehicle before filming began. On rare occasions they forgot to switch the plates, and nobody noticed until after the scene was 'in the can' and it was too late to re-shoot. If you're into details another commercial plate was also used on the Universal Studios Squad. It was 19 542W.

The lettering on the doors and the rear of the Squads also varied with the model of the Dodge. This was in keeping with the letter-

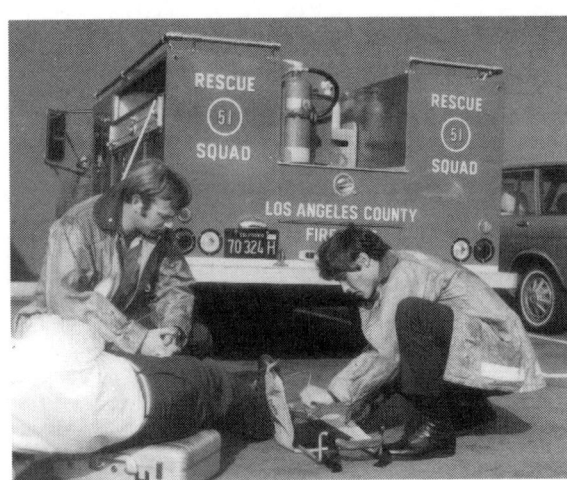

Kevin and Randy
Note the commercial license plate.
Universal Television

ing specs at the time the squad was serviced and repainted if necessary (for the series) by the studio paint shop. The word "paramedic" on the doors of the Squad was put on after series end. No mention is ever made about getting "new" squads in the series, unlike the engine.

A Dodge 100 was used as a "stand-in" for Squad 51, as it was crushed by a jet engine in the *Emergency!* TV movie "Survival on Charter 220." Note the round side mirrors, lack of chrome grab bars on the utility body, and squared-off chrome handles on the 'stand-in' Squad body. Surprisingly enough not one tear was shed by the 'C' Shift medics, or the off-duty Johnny and Roy at the site of their destroyed Squad.

The Squad was donated by Universal Studios to the LA County Fire Department after the series ended and was placed into reserve status. The Commercial Plate was turned in and a "real" tax-exempt plate number, <E>727413, was issued by the DMV, which was used through 1999. It was actually put into service on occasion. (I would like to have seen the faces of those paramedics if they only knew what they were driving). The Squad made brief "guest appearances" *sans* Johnny & Roy, once in a 1977 episode of *CHiPs* and at least one other non-*Emergency!* TV movie.

The 1974 Squad underwent an approximate $30,000 restoration in preparation for its national tour in March 2000. In addition to a new engine, transmission, brake work, and new suspension components, the vehicle received new paint and the lettering design on the doors and rear of the Squad were restored to 1974 specifications. The Squad was literally taken apart down to its axles and put back together. The Museum Association obtained the original TV license plate numbering used in the series from the DMV. No corporate sponsors were obtained for this massive project. Funding was by payroll deductions of the LA County firefighters to the Museum Association, donations from *Emergency!* fans, and the sale of Project 51 items.

The Project 51 tour began on October 17, 1999 in Irvine, California at a daylong kick-off event. The *Emergency!* stars signed autographs, Project 51 items were sold, and the public got their first look at the refurbished Squad. The tour stopped in six more cities

1973 Ward La France
Universal Television

all over the country beginning in March 2000, and ended up in the Smithsonian National Museum of American History in Washington DC on May 16th, 2000. At a private ceremony, several of the key props used in the series such as fire gear, station uniforms, medical equipment, radios, and more were donated to the Museum. The items were accepted into the Smithsonian collection (in the Public Service section), and will be put up for possible exhibit at a future date. The Squad returned to the LA County Fire Museum at 8365 Otis Street in South Gate (Los Angeles) on board its 75' transport after the ceremony.

On February 18, 2002, Randolph Mantooth hosted an event in Los Angeles honoring the first forty LA County paramedics. At the ceremony, held at the Petersen Automotive Museum, the Squad was inducted into its permanent collection. The Museum is located at 6060 Wilshire Blvd. (corner of Fairfax) in Los Angeles.

LA County Engine 60 stationed at Universal Studios. This was an Engine 51 stand in when filming on studio grounds. Photo by author

The first Engine 51 was an in-service 1965, 1250 GPM open-cab Crown Firecoach, Serial number F1400, LACo maintenance vehicle ID number 49215. In service as "Engine 60" it was stationed at Universal Studios (LACo Station 60), and is now located at the LA County Fire Museum in South Gate. Again, adhesive numbers (51) covered the "60" on the doors. Engine 127, sister to engine 60, (with adhesive "51" on the doors) was utilized for stock footage for the pilot, and subsequent shots on location at Station 127, early in the first season. Engine 127 can be seen as Engine 127 in several later episodes. I have no record of what happened to Engine 127.

The Crown's replacement was a 1973 Ward LaFrance Ambassador, Model number P80-1000D-5, serial number 80-811, which was donated to Universal Studios by the manufacturer. LA County took delivery of forty-seven Ward LaFrance engines that year, and Ward wanted their engine to be showcased on the TV program, rather than a Crown. It showed up in the third season in the episode titled

Randy and Kevin in front of Station 51 (Los Angeles County Fire Department 127) with refurbished squad

"The Old Engine." The Ward LaFrance also saw service at the Universal Studio fire station during the off-season and after the series shut down. It was seen in movies (*China Syndrome*), and various TV series shot on the lot or other locations where a fire engine was required for the scene. Sharp eyes could pick out the large 51 still located on the front and side of the engine. In the 1990 TV movie *The Big One: The Great Los Angeles Earthquake*, footage of the emergency services getting ready includes stock footage of Squad 51 and Engine backing in the station.

In 1987, Engine 51 (the Ward) sitting idle on Universal's back lot was put back into service for the Yosemite Concessions Service (YCS) at Yosemite National Park in California. At the time, the Concessions Service was operated by MCA who also owned Universal Studios. That's how the engine ended up in a National Park. Now approaching thirty years old, the engine is still a first-line pumper at the Park, and is staffed by a paid/on call crew of eight firefighters who have full time jobs within the Park.

E-51 in "old" Station 60 in 1975 at Univesal Studios
Photo by author

Originally on a $1.00 a year lease agreement, MCA sold the engine to YCS in 1993 for $5,000. There are no plans at this time to purchase a new engine and return the Ward to LA County's Fire Museum. A few minor modifications have been made to the engine and in keeping with its historical status, Engine 7 as it is now known, is running with license plate, YCS E51.

Yosemite Engine 7
formerly *Emergency!*'s 51
Photo by Captain Ted Farmer
Note the snow chains on the rear tires

Snyder Ambulance of Van Nuys, CA provided many of the ambulances used on *Emergency!* as they did in *Rescue 8*. Magnetic signs were affixed with either "J & R" or "Miller" logos. On rare occasions the signs were left off and "Snyder" would be providing the transport. The ambulance was a 1968 Chevrolet 3500 Series panel-style vehicle. Snyder Unit 33 would be driven to various locations or the Universal lot for the ambulance shots by two off-duty LA City paramedics. They would act as the extras in the load-and-go scenes, also known in the trade as "Swoop & Scoop" and "Scoop & Haul." Ford Super-Duty Econoline vans were used in later episodes. The modular used in the first few episodes was provided by Goodhew/LA and was purchased from Texas. It originally was used in a Fort Worth, Texas funeral home. By the mid 1970s, Modular Ambulance Company was providing the ambulances. The "Miller" ambulance vans showed up again after the series end in the *Emergency!* Movie "Survival on Charter 220."

In crossover appearances, the stars of *Adam-12* appeared in the *Emergency!* pilot as their *Adam-12* characters. Later, the crew of Station 51 is watching a TV episode of *Adam-12* (titled Ambush) on their dayroom TV in the April 8, 1972 "Hang up" episode. In this particular *Adam-12* episode we see the future Dr. Morton, Ron Pinkard, as a police officer. Roy and Johnny run into the *Adam-12* cops at Rampart Hospital, but this time on an October 4, 1972 episode of *Adam-12* titled "Lost and Found." (Strange twist, all this). A bit of trivia for Randolph fans is that he appeared on *Adam-12* in an April 1, 1971 episode titled "Reason to Run," as a drifter suspected of theft. The names Gage, DeSoto, and Stanley were taken from street names in LA. Johnny's badge number is 330, Roy's is 174, and Marco's is 125.

L-R: Kevin Tighe as "Roy," Marco Lopez as "Marco," Mike Norell (holding dog) as "Captain Stanley," Mike Stoker as "Engineer Mike," Tim Donnelly as "Chet," and Randolph Mantooth as "Johnny."
Universal Television

Two "real" LA County Fire Department firefighters on the program were firefighter/specialist Mike Stoker, who drove the engine, and Captain Dick Hammer. Mike retired in 1994 as a Captain after serving for thirty years, and Dick Hammer retired in 1983 after serving for twenty-four years. The photo hanging in the Captain's office is of LA County Fire Department Chief Engineer Richard Houts. Sam Lanier, the dispatching voice of *Emergency!* was a real dispatcher for LA County from 1958 to 1977. Two other members of Station 51 were firefighters Chester B. Kelly and Marco López, who many thought were real LA County firefighters. Both Chet (Tim Donnelly) and Marco (real name) were in several early episodes of *Dragnet* (1967) and *Adam-12*. One confusion people often have about him and his character López said, is that "People always thought that I was a real fireman, probably because I used my real name in the show. That's been a compliment all my life."

Although *Emergency!* (the series) went off the air in 1977, and after years of syndicated reruns titled *Emergency One* or *Emergencia!* in Mexico, *Emergency!* collectibles are still, pardon the pun, HOT. Prices continue to soar on items such as lunchboxes (three styles), medical kits, a board game by Milton Bradley (a French version is also made in Ontario, Canada by Somerville Industries for Milton Bradley), GAF ViewMasters, (in both English and French), puzzles, several types of action accessory kits, comic books (comic book size and in magazine format, four issues each), helmets, (red and the rare yellow and black), survival kits, walkie-talkies, magic slates, a record album, and Johnny & Roy action figures.

In 1975, Fleetwood Toys, Inc. NY, issued a 1:64 scale plastic Engine, Chiefs car, and helicopter with a put-together firehouse, all on a blister card with *Emergency!* photos. For $3.00 you could join Johnny and Roy's "Jr. Paramedic Club." Author Chris Stratton published a novel titled *Emergency!*, based on the TV characters, and published it through Popular Library in 1972. *Emergency!* has produced many collectibles, but neither Kevin Tighe (Roy DeSoto) nor

Randolph Mantooth (John "Johnny" Roderick Gage), or any other cast member benefited from any of the royalties.

There are four *TV Guide* covers with one or more of the cast members with related articles: Julie London, June 17, 1972; Robert Fuller, August 18, 1973; Johnny & Roy, August 3, 1974, & Engine crew and cast, August 16, 1975. There are other regional weekly TV magazines with various cast members shown on the cover with related articles, which came out during the series. These and many other items which collectors have snapped up as rapidly as they appear in collector magazines, such as *The Toy Shop* and on Internet auctions. Scripts and videos from the programs are currently available.

An authorized die-cast version of the squad by Dinky (#267) 1:50 scale, complete with Johnny and Roy plastic figures and a "badge" was released in England in 1979. The L.J. N. Toys Ltd. company of New York released a Squad and an Engine (1:64 scale) labeled "51" in 1975. These were distributed in the "Road*Stars" series with original cast photos on the blister cards, and were authorized by Universal as *Emergency!* toys.

Another version of the Squad was released by Hot Wheels as a red "Emergency Squad" marked "50" in the "Flying Colors" series, bottom stamped 1974, released in 1975. It was also released as the "Ranger Rig" and "Rescue Ranger." It closely resembled the vehicle on *Emergency!* but was not authorized by Universal as such. The Emergency Squad continues to be issued with different card stock, graphics, and stock numbers. To date there are over forty variations of paint schemes and logos to this casting. In 1988, it appeared for the first time with "51" on the side of the squad, then again in 1998 with "Emergency 51" on the side of the "Fire Eater" marked "51," (with a casting date of 1976 on the bottom of the squad). The Fire Eater was also used in a McDonald's promotion without a blister card. This pumper was designed after an American LaFrance engine, not a Ward LaFrance that was on the show.

In recognition of the LA County Fire Department's 75th Anniversary and the 30th Anniversary of paramedics in this country, Code3 Collectibles released a die-cast version of the Crown Firecoach on January 1, 2000. The LA County Fire Department authorized a Limited Edition of 5000 in Code 3's "Classics Series," 1:64 scale, ($34.95). It is identified as Engine 60 (the first Engine 51) that was the actual engine used. It is now sold out and only available on the secondary market. (Code3 issued the Crown with different city locations including LA City and Honolulu later that year).

Hot Wheels (Mattel) also released a LA County FD-approved (their first authorized) Squad 51 in a Special Edition. It was issued in February 2000 with 1974 era Squad logos, 1:64 scale, ($19.95). Ironically, they are using the previous casting originally known as the "Emergency Squad" for this release, still bottom dated 1974. Matchbox (Mattel) was to issue an Emergency Squad in Series 4 of their "Star Car" series in 1999/2000. Only a few 1:64 scale pre-production models were produced with the livery of "Los Angeles County (10) Fire Dept. Rescue Squad" (1974 era lettering) on the doors with 'Emergency!' on the hood. This was to be issue number 24 in the Star Car series. Unknown why they chose squad number 10 or if they were going to change the number to 51 for release.

In April 2001, Code3 Collectibles released in their "Code3 Classic Series" their previously issued Crown as Engine 51 (10,000 units) along with a Squad (20,000 units), and a replica of Station 51 (12 ½" L x 16" W x 4 ½" H), all 1:64 scale. Code3 issued the long awaited 1973 Ward as Engine 51 (15,000 units) in July 2002 to round out the *Emergency!* set. The initial photo on the Code3 site concerned collectors, as the engine sported a full light bar and not the distinctive "gumball" rotator. Code3 advised me that it was a pre-production photo mock-up, and was soon corrected. The photo looked like the engine as it is now in Yosemite National Park as Engine 7. There is even a "talking" Squad; a plush toy, also made by Code3, which emits siren sounds and dispatch tones, which are acknowledged by Johnny Gage, when pressing on the Squad's hood.

At one time the two stars received more fan mail than anybody else at Universal Studios, and the popularity of the series has not waned over the years. The "new" collectibles are evidence of this, as was the October 1998 *Emergency!* '98, The Boys are Back in Town" Convention in Burbank, California. Virtually the entire cast and crew, including stunt people, producers, directors, paramedic technical assistants, with special appearance by Squad 51 and Engine 60, along with a reported 600 to 750 conventioneers, not only from the states but also six foreign countries devoted to *Emergency!*

Bobby Troop and Author Richard Yokley in 1998 at
Emergency! Convention
Photo by LA County FD

attended a fantastic 3-day convention and seminar. I had the distinct honor of presenting Bobby Troup (Dr. Joe Early) with his presentation basket at the awards ceremony.

More trivia: In 1999 *Emergency!* was among the "Top 100 TV Shows of All Time" in a fan-oriented poll conducted by Ultimate TV.

Appearing together again on TV, May 5, 2002, "The Boys" (Randy and Kevin in the audience) were featured on NBC's 75th Anniversary program, along with a clip from the show. *Emergency!* was finally getting its due as one of the network's most memorable shows.

Randy was married on August 10, 2002 with Kevin Tighe as one of the Groomsmen.

Marco López lives near Las Vegas and appears in commercials, still cooks, (see his recipe in a later chapter) and runs a catering business.

Author Richard Yokley in Squad 51 in 1998

CHAPTER THREE — 1970's

A spin-off to the Lassie series was *Lassie's Rescue Rangers*, which aired on ABC from 1973 through 1975. This animated action adventure series kept Lassie in the Forest Service with Head Ranger Ben Turner (voice of Emmy award winning Ted Knight, possibly better known as Ted Baxter on the *Mary Tyler Moore Show*). Along with the Rangers family, the Rescue Rangers included a band of about eight animals, as they struggled to protect the environment and save lives in Thunder Mountain National Park. The Filmation Studio produced the show which aired at 10:00am.

During the run of *Emergency!* the ABC Network, trying to cash in on the popularity of the series, came out in February 1973 with *Firehouse*, a ninety-minute TV Movie of the Week. It starred Vince Edwards (*Ben Casey*) as Firefighter Spike Ryerson, a member of FDNY Engine-23. Although supposedly based in New York, the series was shot in Los Angeles. The movie cutaway with stock fire scenes, and apparatus from New York, Boston, and Cleveland. The storyline revolved around the introduction of a black rookie firefighter, Richard Roundtree (*Shaft*), into an all-white station. He was replacing a white firefighter from Engine 23 recently killed in a fire started by a black arsonist.

The LA City fire station used in the movie is a 75 foot deep single bay station in which the lettering over the bay door is "Engine 23 Truck 5." There is no truck company in the station for the movie. 'Old' 23's station is located at 225 E. 5th Street, Los Angeles. It was taken out of service in 1960, and was a sculptor's studio for a while, but now lies vacant and in a state of disrepair. Built in 1910 for $53,000 dollars, the 3-story station sported two elevators and self-flushing horse stalls. The station does have a New York tie-in, however, as it was used for the interior shots of the firehouse in the 1984 film *Ghostbusters*.

LA County Fire Department Captain Scott Smith provided technical assistance, and played the part of the Battalion Chief. He also provided the engine used in the movie. Metromedia Productions and Richard Berg, President of Stonehenge Productions, produced the TV movie, which was written by Frank Cucci, and directed by Alex March. The 1973 TV movie is available on video and DVD and released in the UK as *"Nightwatch"* and "Feuerwache 23" in Germany.

About a year later, with new writers, and after several rewrites, cast member, and TA changes, the popular LA County Fire Station 8 in West Hollywood was used for a sixty-minute preview pilot for studio executives. The public never saw this film, as it was used to evoke interest in producing a series. It obviously worked as

Firehouse cast
Starring as professional firefighters, ABC-TV's new series debuting Thursday night, January 17,1974. L-R: Bill Overton, James Drury, Brad David (on fire truck), Richard Jaeckel and Michael DeLano. *Firehouse* is a Metromedia Producers Corporation/Stonehenge production.

Firehouse, now not only filmed in Los Angeles, but also as LA City Fire Station 23, made its debut in January 1974 as a mid-season replacement airing at 8:30pm on Thursdays. Without the heavy racial overtones, the half-hour series airing against *The Waltons* starred James Drury, in his first series since *The Virginian*, as Captain Spike Ryerson on Engine 23.

Firehouse TV Series - 1974
L-R: Actor Michael Delano, Technical Advisor Captain Jim Perry and Actor Richard Jaeckel
ABC Photo

Drury got his feet wet doing ride-a-longs with the Shreveport Louisiana Fire Department once he knew the series was to begin. Drury stated, "We're dealing with true Americans, heroes who walk through hell to put a fire out." Vince Edwards and Richard Roundtree were no longer members of the cast. In fact Richard Jaeckel (*Emergency!* 2.2) was the only one to survive the crew change from the TV movie to the series. The TA for the movie, Scott Smith (*Emergency!* 1.4) was on set during filming, but not as the TA. Scott would drive his old rig (from the movie) when used, and would fill in as "atmosphere." The series TA, Captain Jim Perry, from LA City Fire Department also did some on-camera work in a rescue or fire scene. He carried "victims" down a ladder, and slid the lifeline at the tower, which was part of the trailer they used. He also had short command-type lines on the radio. The series ran a full 13-episode season (including reruns) through August. The producers (and cast) hoped it would be expanded to a sixty-minute series if picked up in September for the 1974/1975 season.

Brad David (l) is rookie fireman Billy Danzell and James Drury is his hardnosed Captain, Spike Ryerson, in in the dramatic adventure series, *Firehouse*.
ABC Photo

Fire station location shots for the series utilized an in-service station in posh Beverly Hills - Fire Station 2, located at 1100 Coldwater Canyon Drive. New engines were not used, the Fire Department Technical Advisor would drive a reserve 1960 vintage LA City open cab Crown Firecoach Apparatus, from Fire Station 99 (where he worked) to the set at 20th Century Fox and other locations as required. Another engine used in the series was an open-cab Crown Firecoach Hi-Pressure Hose Wagon, which was given to the La Paz, Baja, California, Mexico Fire Department (on a Sister City program), and is still in service. As previously mentioned they would also use Smith's engine from the pilot on occasion.

Los Angeles City hi-pressure hose wagon. This is similar to what was used in *Firehouse*.
Photo by Larry Ford, LAFD Retired nd Crown Firecoach Enthusiast

Metromedia Productions produced the 1974 series, with Richard Berg, who was one of three executive producers. The January 13, 1974 issue of *TV Weekly* from the LA Herald-Examiner featured James Drury on the cover, in fire gear, with a related article and photos about the series. The April 7, 1974 issue of S. Middlesex MA *TV Viewer* ran a photo of James Drury in fire gear with an article. Pennsylvania's *TV Time and Channel TV guide* for March 30-April 5, 1974 had James Drury and Richard Jaeckel on the cover. Well-known TV critic, Cleveland Amory, posted a review of *Firehouse* in the May 4-10, 1974 issue of *TV Guide*. It was announced in the same issue that *Firehouse* would not be renewed for the fall season. The May 18, 1974 issue of *TV Guide* featured an article with two pages of photos of a fire stunt sequence filmed in Topanga Canyon. The series also aired in Israel in 1977.

A spin-off of *Emergency!* was a cartoon series ***Emergency! + 4***, which aired on NBC at 9:30am September 8, 1973 through September 4, 1976 with twenty-three original episodes. Produced and directed by Fred Calvert for Universal TV, Mark VII Ltd., and Fred Calvert Production Companies, the series had Johnny and Roy continuing their life-saving roles with the assistance of four kids and their pets. Kevin and Randolph did the voiceovers for their animated characters. *Emergency! + 4* collectibles include coloring books, activity books, and a "press-out and play" activity box produced in 1975 by Emergency Productions, and a camera and Halloween costume.

During 1974 on NBC's Saturday morning program, ***Go, Emergency!*** stars Kevin and Randy made a guest appearance. Aimed at children, and hosted by Greg Morris from *Mission Impossible,* the program explored various occupations. The *Emergency!* stars talked about the paramedics of LA County's Rescue Squads. *Go* aired from 1973 to 1976, and was produced by George A. Heinemann.

The Rangers
L-R: Kevin Tighe, Colby Chester, Randolph Mantooth, James Richardson, and unidentified, in the *Rangers*. Universal Television Photo

Sierra debuted September 12, 1974 on NBC. This sixty-minute, 13-episode series (only 11 were completed) was filmed in Yosemite National Park, known as Sierra National Park in the series. Airing against *The Walton's* on Thursdays at 8:00pm, this was a program about Park Rangers, and their dealings with lost hikers, enforcement of park regulations, coping with visitors, and search and rescue operations. John Denver wrote the *Sierra* theme song. Yosemite's Chief Ranger Jack Morehead served as the show's Technical Advisor. Special effects coordinator was Mel Arnold.

The ninety-minute pilot for *Sierra*, which in an unusual move aired two weeks after the series ended, was titled **The Rangers**. It revolved around the rescue operations of the Park Rangers, and aired on December 24, 1974. Although neither are "fire" programs they are included here because Kevin Tighe and Randolph Mantooth appear in the pilot as their *Emergency!* characters. In a mountain training exercise DeSoto hurts himself in a fall while climbing a cliff, and is transported in a National Park Service station wagon.

An injured Roy DeSoto in a scene from *The Rangers*. Universal Television

A probable *Emergency!* spin-off as it was produced by *Emergency!* alumni; R. A. Cinader wrote the pilot, Ed Self produced, and Jack Webb was Executive Producer for Mark VII Ltd., and Universal TV. James G. Richardson, who starred as Paramedic-Park Ranger Tim Cassidy, later appeared in three episodes of *Emergency!* In 1976 and 1977, he wrote two of the episodes as Paramedic Craig "by-the-book" Brice. Unlike *Sierra*, almost the entire cast of *The Rangers* appeared in several episodes of *Adam-12* and/or *Emergency!*. Richardson was the only one retained for the series

Sierra. According to co-producer Hannah Shearer (also from *Emergency!*) 32-year-old Harrison Ford was one of five actors on the short-list for the second lead part in the *Sierra* series. The part ultimately went to Ernest Thompson (*On Golden Pond*), who replaced Colby Chester as Ranger Matt Harper.

Ford, who had boyhood dreams of becoming a forest ranger, insisted that his success as a leading man came primarily from a lapse in public taste. In an October 2000 interview with *World Entertainment News*, Ford said he doesn't want to play bit parts because he sees himself as a fireman, and only wants to put out the biggest fires possible. He explains, "A lapse in public taste led me to become a leading man, and I take advantage of that opportunity. I'm like a fireman. When I go out on call, I want to put out a big fire, I don't want to put out a fire in a dumpster. Not some trash fire." Three years after Ford lost out on *Sierra*, he became Han Solo.

On March 1, 1975, during season four of *Emergency!* a pilot titled ***905-Wild*** was aired. The title refers to the police code for "Wild Animal Loose, Threatening." The *Emergency!* spin-off starred Mark Harmon (later seen in *240-Robert* and *The Presidio*), and Albert Popwell (two *Dirty Harry* movies) as Paramedic-Animal Control Officers, and was directed by Jack Webb for Mark VII and Universal Television Productions. This would be Webb's only directorial role for the series. *Emergency!* episode 4.23 opens with Johnny and Roy responding to a medical call in a suburban canyon area for a "man down, bleeding." They discover a Bengal tiger on the premises, and hence call Animal Control. Later, a brush fire threatens the area, and Animal Control is confronted with rescuing several animals, including an elephant. Rampart Hospital becomes a veterinary surgical center, with Dr. Brackett operating on an injured goat, with instructions via telephone from Animal Control's head veterinarian. The show also starred David Huddleston as the

Mark Harmon and Albert Popwell in "905 Wild" on *Emergency!*
Universal Television Photo

vet, and Gary Crosby (*Adam-12*) as head of the Los Angeles Bureau of Animal Control. Rose Ann Zecker (a.k.a. Rose Ann Deel) is the unit secretary. The network never picked up the proposed thirty-minute series listed by *TV Guide* as "an NBC program in development."

In 1977, a new NBC Programming Executive and former head of CBS Records, Irwin Segelstien, wanted to cancel *Emergency!* and replace it with ***Pine Canyon is Burning***. The same producers, writers, and directors from *Emergency!* developed the pilot for MCA/Universal TV, which aired on May 18, 1977. Produced with the cooperation of the Los Angeles County Fire Department, it starred Kent McCord (*Adam-12*) as a Paramedic and Captain of LA County Fire Station 110. As a widowed firefighter with two children, he transfers to a one-man fire/rescue/brush station in the Los Angeles foothills, Patrol Station 99 in Pine Canyon, in order to be home at night with his two children. McCord's daughter, Megan, plays his daughter in the movie. McCord replaces a veteran Captain who is retiring from Pine Canyon station, played by Andrew Duggan. Another Captain in the movie on Engine 78 (formerly Engine 51, the Ward), Larry Delaney, also appeared in *The Rangers* and *Emergency!*

Station 110 is an actual LA County fire station, which houses two boats, a pumper, and truck. The opening scenes were filmed on location at Station 110, 4433 Admiralty Way, Marina Del Rey. Patrol station 99 was also a real station in the Angeles National Forest, which is no longer in service, and now a private residence. The station used was "old" Patrol Station 77 at 47376 Ridge Route, near the intersection of Ridge Route and Pine Canyon Road, located east of the town of Gorham on Interstate 5 on the "Grapevine," a long way from Malibu where other scenes were filmed. The Patrol 99 vehicle was a 4-wheel drive "mini-pumper" (with the vehicle manufacturer ID duct taped over for the movie).

The series was not developed, *Emergency!* was eventually canceled (even with a 28 share at that time), and Segelstein was gone six months later. *Emergency!* would go on to film six made-for-TV movies, but with only Kevin Tighe and Randolph Mantooth reprising their paramedic roles from the series, along with the hospital staff of Julie London, Robert Fuller, Ron Pinkard, and Bobby Troup in the two LA-based movies.

A series involving the combined efforts of fire, police, and the ocean rescue departments on "Channel Island" off the coast of Southern California was titled ***Code-R***. The team battled arsonists, muggers, vehicle accidents, bootleggers, water rescues, and more

TV Firefighters

L-R: Marty Kove, Tom Simcox and James Houghton co-starred in *CODE-R*. CBS Photo

on a weekly basis. The series aired on CBS Fridays at 8:00pm during January through June 1977, with thirteen sixty-minute episodes. The series starred Martin Kove (*Code Red*) as the Head Life Guard, Tom Simcox (*Emergency!* 3.7) as the Police Chief, and James Houghton as the Fire Chief.

The doctor played by Tom Williams also appeared in *Emergency!* episodes 6.21 and 7.3. *Code-R* was created and produced by Edwin

Tim Simcox, Susanne Reed, James Houghton and Marty Kove in *CODE-R*. CBS Photo

Marty Kove, Susanne Reed, James Houghton and Tom Simcox in CODE-R. CBS Photo

Self at Warner Brothers Studios. Self produced the third and fourth seasons of *Emergency!* and also directed several episodes. He also produced *The Rangers*. The February 13-19, 1977 St. Louis Post Dispatch *TV Magazine* featured Suzanne Reed, "Suzy," as the dispatcher, on the cover, with a related article. *TV Guide* ran an article in the March 5-11, 1977 issue. Music was composed by Lee Holdridge (*Pine Canyon is Burning* and *The Rangers*). Notable guest stars were Pamela Susan Shoop (*Emergency!* 6.4) on 4-15-77, and Cheryl Ladd in the last episode on 6-3-77.

240-Robert, which aired from 1979-1981, followed the exploits of the Los Angeles County Sheriff's Department Emergency Services Detail, primarily a Search & Rescue unit. Utilizing helicopters, boats, and a customized Ford Bronco, the three-members of the team were certified SCUBA divers, skilled mountain climbers, and licensed paramedics, in addition to being full-time law enforcement officers, who managed to extract citizens from dangerous situations. *240-Robert* featured John Bennett Perry as Deputy Theodore

Roosevelt Applegate, III or "Trap," Mark Harmon as Deputy Dwayne Thibideaux or "Thib," and Joanna Cassidy as Deputy Morgan Wainwright, the helicopter pilot of the unit, and the first woman to be accepted and assigned to the Emergency Services Detail (ESD). It was often compared to *Emergency!* because of its similar story lines of rescuing scuba divers, emergency surgeries, hi-rise rescues, vehicle accident rescues, and of course rescuing beautiful women.

The sixty-minute series was based on a real-life paramedic 240 unit of the LA Sheriff's Department. The producers were granted exclusive privileges to adapt actual case histories from ESD files, as well as use of the Sheriff Dept badge, seal, and uniform. At the time, there were no female members of the "real" Emergency Services Detail. Rick Rosner, executive producer and a reserve sheriff's deputy with a rescue unit, created *240-Robert* and *CHiPs*. Filmways Pictures and Rosner Television produced the series for Orion Television airing on ABC. The 13-episode series first aired on December 3, 1979. In season two, Mark Harmon and Joanna Cassidy left the show, but Stephen W. Burns and Pamela Hensley (*Emergency!* 3.17) were introduced as Deputy Brett Cueva and Deputy Sandy Harper, who took over as the chopper pilot. Only three episodes were filmed with this group, all airing in March 1981, ending the series.

Many of the episodes were directed by Christian I. Nyby II (*Emergency! Pine Canyon is Burning, The Rangers, CHiP's,* and *Adam-12*), and others by Bruce Kessler, (*Code-R*). The Fall Preview Edition of *TV Guide* for September 8, 1979, featured a photo and story. The Canadian version of *TV Guide* ran a cover feature on Joanna Cassidy on November 3-9, 1979. The St. Louis Post Dispatch's *TV Magazine* did a cover feature on Mark Harmon on September 30, 1979. (Although not a "fire" program, *240-Robert* is included as the team members are Emergency Service Paramedics).

This show is not to be confused with *Chopper One*, which aired five years before *240-Robert* in 1974. A mid-season replacement, which aired January through July 1974 on ABC, it followed the exploits of a Southern California based police chopper team, the Western California Police Department, and starred Dirk Benedict (*Battlestar Galactica* and *The 'A' Team*). A Spelling and Lee Goldberg production with RKO Radio Pictures produced this thirty-minute 13-episode series, which immediately preceded James Drury's *Firehouse*.

Two years after *Chopper One* but before *240-Robert*, a program with a similar premise was produced in Australia. It was titled *Chopper Squad,* and began with a ninety-minute movie pilot in 1976. I include this program because the story line also dealt with a Search and Rescue unit, much like *240-Robert,* even down to the vehicles used in the program. It was filmed primarily along Sydney's North Beach, or inland as the story required. The sixty-minute series began in 1978, and ran for two seasons with twenty-six episodes. Collectibles produced by Corgi were a Bell Jet Ranger 2 helicopter (1:43 scale), a Boat, and a Surf Rescue Jeep, all with *Chopper Squad* logos. The same vehicles were released in the Corgi Jr. line.

CHAPTER FOUR — THE 1980's

On September 20, 1981, on ABC a ninety-minute pilot called *Code Red* aired. Created by Laurence Heath (*Hawaii 5-0, Murder She Wrote*), it was a story about an LA City firefighting family and arson investigators. The pilot, written by Heath, was shot in late March with a $2,000,000 budget, and a working title of *Pumper 1*. It continued with 18 sixty-minute episodes, which premiered on November 1, 1981. The series, touted as a dramatic informational/educational series, ran through July 1982 (against *60 Minutes*), with original stories, and concluded in September with reruns.

Sam Jones, Martina Deignan, Andrew Stevens
ABC Photo

The series revised its format from the movie for younger viewers. The pilot starred Lorne Green (*Bonanza*) as Captain Joe Rorchek of the LAFD Arson unit; he would become a Battalion Chief for the series. The Chief's family included two sons, one a firefighter, Andrew Stevens, and the other a LAFD Helicopter pilot, Sam

Jones. Adam Rich (*Eight is Enough*) joined the cast after the pilot episode. He portrayed a 14-year-old LAFD Explorer Scout fostered by the Chief's family, and was adopted in the fourteenth episode.

Martina Deignan as the female lead, riding tailboard on the engine, represented LA City's newly graduated and first female firefighter, formerly a City paramedic. (It is interesting to note here that LA City did not recruit female firefighters until 1983, two years after the program aired. Two completed the academy in February 1984, and both left the job in the mid 90's. The first actual "documented" female firefighter served in 1912 with a volunteer company working for the Los Angeles Fire Department).

Code Red was produced by Irwin Allen (*Towering Inferno*) at Columbia Pictures Studios with the approval and assistance of the LAFD. John Guillermin (*Towering Inferno*) directed many episodes. Technical Advisor for the series was a retired LAFD

Martina Deignan as Haley Green in *Code Red*
ABC Photo

Andrew Stevens in *Code Red*
ABC Photo

Battalion Chief, Joe S. Webber. Fire station location shots used LA City Station 49 at 400 Yacht St. at Berth 194 in Wilmington (in the area of San Pedro), designated as Station 1 for the pilot and series. Station 49 houses LAFD Boat 3 and 4, one engine, and a Battalion Chief.

The featured Engine was a new E-One, (Emergency One, Inc), as P1 (Pumper 1, hence the working title), and a Crown 50 foot Snorkel as W1 (Wagon 1). The snorkel was actually an in-service engine assigned to Station 49. Also responding out of *Code Red*'s Station 1, which housed sixteen firefighters, was a tillered aerial rounding out the "Task Force 1" assignment. A Helicopter and a fireboat responded as required, and also were actual in-service equipment. Helicopter 4 was used for the pilot, and Chopper 6 was used in the series. A two-year-old Dalmatian named Sophie, who also rode tailboard, rounded out the crew.

The home of Chief Rorcheck (Lorne Green) was not on Columbia's back lot, but in a real residential area in the 1000 Block of North Banning Blvd. in Wilmington, not far from Station 49. Aimed at young viewers, *Code Red* aired at 7:00pm on Sundays, and each episode ended with an educational fire prevention talk and life saving themes. In 1983 the Young Artist Awards nominated Adam Rich for Best Young Actor in a Drama Series. Eleven-year-old Kirk Cameron (*Growing Pains*) made his first TV series appearance in *Code Red*. Tony Award winner Robert Alda, who played Dr. Brooks in the pilot episode, was also in *Emergency!* 2.16. Lorne Green could not shake the patriarch image of *Bonanza*, and thus *Code Red* was also known as "*Bonanza* with Red Lights and Siren." Even Battlestar Galactica was known as "*Bonanza* in Space." If you wanted to call Chief Joe Rorchek's home, you would need to dial 555-2364. The house was at 9876 Temple Lane. A combination of low ratings and an actors strike kept this series from returning for a second season.

Firefighting Family

(clockwise from bottom)

Julie Adams, Sam J. Jones, Martina Deignan, Andrew Stevens, and Lorne Greene in *Code Red.* ABC Photo

In 1981, Columbia Pictures Industries authorized Matchbox (Lesney UK) to produce a series of eight die-cast 1:64 scale models for the series *Code Red.* A Fire engine, Snorkel engine, Sky Buster SB-20/SB-25 helicopter, chief's car, fire boat, all with "Los Angeles City Fire Department" tampos, (the boat and helicopter are numbered "4," which were the numbers of the actual equipment used in the pilot), LAPD car and motorcycle, and a "box" ambulance, which reads "Pacific Ambulance" on the sides, all which featured the cast of *Code Red* on the blister pack cardstock. In the same year, the Processed Plastic Company in Illinois released a twenty-eight inch long "*Code Red* Hook and Ladder" with six firefighter figures, and a photo of the cast. The truck also had a three-piece extendable rotating ladder, which reached thirty-six inches.

Other *Code Red* collectibles are a Firefighter, Paramedic, and Fire Investigator kits, and a bag of plastic firefighters, produced by the Imperial Toy Corp. in 1981, all with photos of the cast members on the packaging. In 1981, Revel produced 1:32 scale model "snap kits" for the Fire Chief's car, a Chevy Nova, (although in the series he drove a Ford Crown Victoria), a Fire Rescue Chopper #6, and an Ambulance. The September 1981 issue of *Going Places* featured the cast of *Code Red* on the cover, along with Lorne's TV wife, Julie Adams, and a related story. In *TV Guide,* a cast photo appeared in the September 1981 Fall Preview edition and articles appeared in the February 13th and 20th, 1982 editions.

On September 23, 1986, CBS aired **Firefighter**, a made-for-TV movie, in their "Read More About It" program. Based on the true story of Cindy Fralick, the first female firefighter in the Los Angeles County Fire Department. Applying in 1982, along with 6,000 men, Cindy graduated the academy on February 13, 1983. The plot line details the prejudice and hostility during her training period eventually winning the respect of her male counterparts. Nancy McKeon starred and co-produced the 96 minute autobiographical story filmed in West Vancouver, British Columbia at Fire Station 41. The movie also starred Barry Corbin (*Northern Exposure*), and James Whitmore Jr. as Fire Captains. Directed by Robert M. Lewis, and adapted by Kathryn Montgomery from Fralick's autobiography. *The Greater Alarm* was the production's working title and Cindy's idea. "A greater alarm is a 'big deal fire' and 'quite alarming,' and having a female on the fire department is a big deal and quite alarming to many," states Fralick. Cindy Fralick, who became a paramedic, is currently a Captain with the LA County Fire Department.

Produced with the cooperation of the Los Angeles County Fire Department (LACoFD). Technical Advisors LACoFD Captain Pat Bradshaw and Captain Barbee. Fralick was often on hand to view the filming and offer advice when necessary. Produced by Forest Hills Productions in association with Embassy Television.

Cindy was one of the first 13 women featured on *Cool Women* in 2000 on the WE Networks '*Romance Classics*' division. The program was dedicated to celebrating some of society's unsung heroes by exploring their achievements and examining their motivations. It was produced by award winning director, producer, actress, and choreographer, Debbie Allen.

A reality-based series featuring actual scenes interspersed with reenactments of police, firefighters, paramedics, and ordinary citizens "risking their lives to save others" is the TV series *Rescue 911*. The show was hosted by William Shatner, (*Star Trek, T.J. Hooker*), who did the standup and segment lead-ins from the Huntington Beach Fire Department in California. Arnold Shapiro Productions, in association with CBS Entertainment Productions, produced the sixty-minute series, which aired on CBS at 8:00pm on Tuesdays. The series was developed and supervised by Norman S. Powell, Sr. Vice President of production for CBS. It previewed September 5 and premiered September 19, 1989, airing in over sixty countries worldwide from 1989 through 1996, and continues to air in syndication in the US and around the world.

Rescue 911 earned several awards over the years, including a People's Choice Award in 1990 and a Media Excellence Award. *Rescue 911* was considered for an Emmy in 1993 but was not nominated, although it did receive a Certificate of Merit from the American Red Cross. However, more important than awards, the show is directly credited with having saved the lives of over 300 men, women, children, and animals during its initial airing. *Rescue 911* spawned many worldwide imitations. It can still be seen in syndication in some areas, currently on cable and dish providers, and on the Hallmark Entertainment Network several times weekly.

TV Firefighters

Fire/rescue-related collectibles for *Rescue 911* includes a set of 5 die-cast vehicles produced by Matchbox in 1990. The set features a Fire Observer Van, a 1:62 scale ambulance, a doctor's/medic car, a police cruiser, and a 1:64 scale pace car, all with flashing lights and sirens. At least three CBS Inc. authorized books, *Rescue 911 Kid Heroes* (1992), *Extraordinary Stories - Rescue 911* (1993), and *Rescue 911 – Animal Rescues* (1995) were published. In 1993, AMT/ERTL released a 1:25 scale Ford Taurus police car, 1:48 scale Helicopter, and a 1:25 scale Dodge Tradesman ambulance van. Also in 1993 Marchon MR-1 produced two HO scale race sets "*Rescue 911* Chopper Rescue," and "Police Pursuit." A "World's Greatest Rescues" video featuring rescues from around the world, as well as other related videos of stories not aired were produced. The Toy Group, Inc. of Westhampton Beach, New York, in 1993, produced a Search & Rescue Team die-cast metal and plastic set, with four emergency vehicles based on the TV show. There is a Jeep, helicopter, car, and a van. Also included are 911 stickers for the telephone. The Ja-Ru Toy Co. of Jacksonville, FL issued an Air Rescue set featuring 4 firefighters and a *Rescue 911* helicopter dated 1993 CBS Inc., and manufactured in China. In 1994, Ja-Ru also produced a "Squirt Extinguisher" squirt gun and a "*Rescue 911* Outdoor Set" with canteen, axe, compass, and other items.

William Shatner, host of *Rescue 911*, a reality-based series featuring actual scenes of police, firefighters, and paramedics risking their lives to save others.
CBS Photo

In 1994, Gottlieb manufactured a full-size pinball machine for *Rescue 911* with fire engines, ambulances, and a helicopter, which flies and picks up the ball. Also in 1994, CBS authorized the licensing of clothing, such as t-shirts, baseball caps, and other items, and a red plastic Rescue 911 Fireman's hat with show label front piece, manufactured by Collegeville in 1995. *TV Guide* ran at least three articles about the show, the Fall Preview Edition of September 9, 1989, as well as February 10-16, 1990, and April 9-15, *1994. Total TV* ran an article in its August 13-19, 1994 issue. The Canadian *TV Scene* Magazine ran a cover and article in the August 15, 1992 issue published by the *Evening Program*.

My department was briefly considered for a rescue segment due to the uniqueness of the incident. We were working a 1st alarm residential structure fire when I was notified by dispatch of a possible cardiac arrest, two houses away from our fire. Further advised that the patient was "on the roof". I pulled one of my firefighters aside, told him of the situation, to grab the equipment and check it out, and that I would have the next due engine assist. My firefighter reported that we indeed have a full cardiac arrest on the roof of the house and began CPR. He was up there, according to his wife, to wet down his shake shingle roof to prevent it from catching fire if an ember from the structure fire went his way. The scene was lit up by the Sheriff's helicopter powerful night scope as it was late in the evening. Several shocks were delivered via AED to the patient, "on the roof", prior to medics arrival at which time the patient was lowered to the ground and turned over to the medics. As unique as this incident was the producers did not utilize it for their program as Rescue 911 typically broadcasts successful outcomes. Sadly, the man later died in the hospital.

CHAPTER FIVE — THE 1990's

H.E.L.P. first aired on Saturday March 3, 1990 (a late mid-season replacement), and stood for ***Harlem Eastside Lifesaving Program.*** The sixty-minute pilot and 6-episode ABC series was filmed on location in New York, and depicted stories of firefighters, Emergency Service Unit (ESU) police officers, and city paramedics working together out of the same facility in New York City's Harlem. In this short-lived series they coaxed an escaped cougar out of a building, confronted a mad bomber in the subway, coaxed a jumper off a bridge, dealt with rat infestations during a garbage strike, natural gas explosions, and removed terrified residents out of burning buildings.

It starred John Mahoney (*Emergency!* 2:19, *Frasier*) as Deputy Chief Patrick Meacham (Irish of course), a twenty-nine year veteran of the FDNY, who is in charge of the unit formed in the fall of 1989 as a pilot program for the city. *H.E.L.P.* also featured David Caruso (*N.Y.P.D. Blue, CSI-Miami*), as a Police Officer in the pilot episode only, and John Spencer (*The West Wing*) as a firefighter and close friend of the Chief.

H.E.L.P. introduced newcomers 28-year-old Wesley Snipes as a Police Officer in his first TV starring role, and 23-year-old Marjorie Monaghan as a firefighter. According to Marjorie, "They'd shot the pilot like a year before and they'd added two female roles and they were casting those. And I got it. So my first professional gig was a television series called *H.E.L.P.*" Ironically Marjorie is seen in the opening credits of the pilot (the untitled episode one), but doesn't appear in the program until episode two. There were several cast member changes, due to the difference in time of filming the pilot and the remaining six episodes. Along with Marjorie there are different EMS personnel and John Spencer came on board in episode two. Spencer would go on to *LA Law* for four years after filming *H.E.L.P.* One episode guest starred 10-year-old Christina Ricci (*Sleepy Hollow*) portraying a 6-year-old who delivers her mother's baby. A continual theme in the series was the Chief's ill daughter, who needs a liver transplant, and his thoughts about writing a book about life in the fire service.

The *H.E.L.P.* firefighters wore the number "19" (red on a black insert, which is not a FDNY color scheme) on their helmet fronts. (In actuality Engine 19 was a Manhattan engine disbanded in 1947). The fire station location for the series called "The Barn" was filmed in East Harlem, in a vacant three story brick auto body shop at 505 East 116th Street, between Pleasant Avenue and FDR Drive.

Outside of *H.E.L.P.* quarters on E. 116th Street
L-R: Lt. Mike Quinn L-30, Fireman Bob Meissner E-59, Fireman Rich Kathman E-59, and Fireman Keith Nicoliello L-30
Today the building is a working auto repair shop.
Photo courtesy of Keith Nicoliello

TV Firefighters

All the interior sets such as the dispatch center, day room, and Chief's office etc, were constructed on the site. The site is currently used as an auto repair, car stereo installation, and window tinting facility. The *H.E.L.P.* logo painted on the far right gray rollup door is no longer visible. Gray was the background color of the logo, so they simply painted over the logo with gray paint when filming ceased. Since the pilot was filmed sometime earlier a different location was used; a building on the NW corner of E. 59th Street and 1st Avenue, under the 59th Street Bridge, also known as the Queensboro Bridge.

Engines and ladders used for the series were out of FDNY's reserve fleet, located at the FDNY training center on Randalls Island, commonly referred to as "The Rock." Reserve unit 510, a 1980 ALF engine became Engine 507 in the series, and a 1980 Mack CF Tower Ladder as Ladder 2 were "loaned" to the production company. Also used were a 1980, or earlier, Seagrave rear mount as Ladder 16 in the pilot, and then renumbered to Ladder 546 in the series, and a Seagrave tiller as Ladder 54. FDNY's Unit 435, a Heavy Duty tow truck was also used.

FDNY firefighters were hired as MPO's, chauffeurs, tillermen, and extras. Members of Engine 59 / Ladder 30 (The Harlem Zoo) featured prominently in the pilot and series. From Ladder 30 there was John "Bunker" Murrey and Gene Kananowicz; from Engine 59 were Bob Meissner, Rich Pagona, and Rich Kathman, who all have since retired. Still active is

"Real" fireman, Keith Nicoliello L-30 and Tom Bresnahan who played firefighter Jimmy Ryan in *H.E.L.P.*
Photo courtesy Keith Nicoliello

firefighter Keith "Nick" Nicoliello, still at Ladder 30. At the time a Lt. at Ladder 30, but now a Battalion Chief in Queens is Mike Quinn, and Lt. Andrew "The Moose" Bainton at Engine 59. Lt. Bainton was the liaison between the production company and the FDNY, arranging firefighter extras and equipment for the series.

The PD, Fire, and EMS personnel all wore distinctive *H.E.L.P.* patches, although they differed slightly in each agency. Chief Meacham (John Mahoney), although wearing the rank of Deputy Chief on his collar, is identified as "Captain Mecham" in the opening credits. Actual address locations of incidents are used in the series. The only thing slightly out of sync is the arrival of Battalion 28 in a couple of the fire incidents. Battalion 28 covers the northeast area of Brooklyn. In the pilot, the distinctive two-tone fire alarm from *Emergency!* is heard over the radio, while dispatching units to an incident.

One story that came out of the filming comes from Nick (at Ladder 30), a tillerman during the series. "On one particular shoot I was working with fellow fireman John "Bunker" Murrey. At 6' 4" and 300 pounds he is a giant of a man. Well, we were just supposed to move a tiller ladder truck, him in the front on the tractor and me at the tiller. Well, we waited, waited, and waited. Different production problems, then it was the weather that stopped us from working.

But for John, he was in heaven, a large gourmet breakfast that morning, followed by a great lunch, afternoon snack, followed by a glutinous dinner, then a late night pizza party. By wrap-up time one of the directors commented that not only was it a waste of money, production wise (that day), but that big guy (John) cost us a bundle in food."

Executive producers and co-creators, Christopher Crowe (*Miami Vice, Seven Days*) and Dick Wolf (*Miami Vice, Law & Order*) were

TV Firefighters

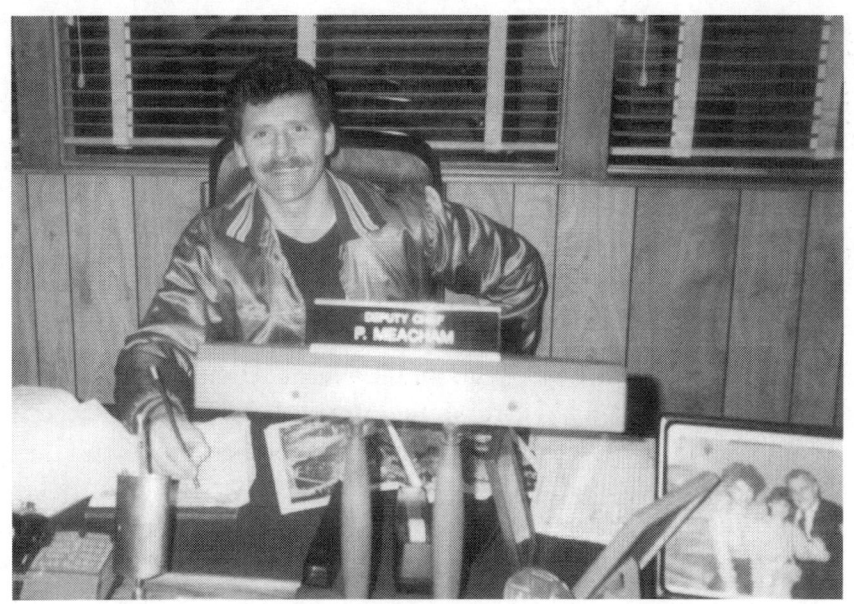

Fireman Keith Nicoliello L30 clowning on the set of H.E.L.P.
Photo taken in Chief Mecham's office - note the family
photo on the desk.
Photo by Nick Nicoliello

both credited with writing the pilot. Michael Rauch produced the show for ABC Productions, Universal TV, and Wolf Films, titled *Das Rettungsteam Im Einsatz* in Germany (*The Rescue Team in Action*), and *S.O.S in New York* in Latin American countries. The series was shown in France and throughout Europe during 1992. Original theme music was by Oscar winner Jerry Goldsmith, along with his son, Joel, who scored the episodes. *H.E.L.P.* has also been available in England in PAL format.

Similarities with another program and a movie: If you never saw this short-lived series just think *Third Watch*. About the only difference is that they (the *H.E.L.P.* crew) are all working out of the same building. As in *Third Watch* the paramedics and PD take up about 85% of the story, while fire the remaining 15%. The pilot storyline is about an influential business-man who was recently honored by the Fire Department's benevolent society as "NYFD 1989 Man of the Year." (That is not a typo on my part – On the banner at the party and on the sash of the honoree it is 'NYFD') Unbeknownst to the Fire Department at the time, he owns tenement buildings in Harlem, and is having them burned down for insurance purposes, wherein two of the *H.E.L.P.* firefighters are killed. Chief Meacham finally arrests him after confronting him at a party – does 1991's *Backdraft* sound familiar?

There is in fact a H.E.L.P. Team in the FDNY. Unlike its depiction in the TV series, it is part of the Bureau of Health Services. Established in 1981, its purpose is to assist members and their families, both active and retired, when admitted to hospital. The H.E.L.P. team members insure the patients receive appropriate care, and assist with other family concerns.

The Fox Network presented **Code 3**, which aired from 1992-1994 with a total of sixty-five episodes. It was their version of *Rescue 911* without the recreations, and was hosted by Gil Gerard (*Buck Rogers in the 25th Century*), and created by John Langley (*Cops*) for Barbour/Langley Productions. Like *Cops*, also by the Barbour/Langley team, the show involved riding along with actual firefighters in various cities throughout the US. It aired on various days and times during its initial airing beginning April 11, 1992. Paul Suchecki was writer and field producer, Steve Gerbson directed, and Peter Rosten and Doug Waterman produced. *Code 3* can still be seen in syndication in some areas. Theme music was by Jack Tiller and Arcangelo Faiella.

Philly Heat, a sixty-minute pilot for ABC, which aired Saturday July 1, 1995 at 10:00pm. The show was a firefighting drama about Philadelphia firefighters who face danger on the job, and other problems when off duty. Filmmakers lived with and rode along with Philadelphia's real Engine 50, and onboard a second similarly painted Engine 50, manned by actors and off-duty firefighters from

Philadelphia's IAFF Local 22. They actually worked the fires, and footage of them operating on the fire ground and other emergencies was filmed.

During time between alarms, response scenes aboard the apparatus, and drive by shots were filmed along with many close-ups of the principals in action. The footage was then processed and printed, and given to the show's writers, who scripted stories around these incidents. In the fall of 1993, dialog was filmed on a sound stage built in a warehouse along the Delaware River. In *Philly Heat*, the already filmed file incidents drove the dialog and storylines.

Peter Boyle (The father from *Everybody Loves Raymond*) played the cigar-smoking Battalion Chief. Boyle, a Vietnam veteran and Fire Marshal, suddenly has to step into the job of Battalion Commander of the cities busiest station (and it really is). Boyle drove a Suburban done up in Philly FD colors. At the time they were still using station wagons and Broncos for their BC's. Julianne Margulies portrayed a firefighter/medic assigned to (the fictitious) Rescue 50. There is no actual rescue unit assigned to Station 50. Currently Engine 50 is housed with Ladder 12 and Medic 22. Margulies thinks that firemen are the "hunkiest" of the medical support group. "They can swing you onto their shoulder with one arm and carry you down a ladder." Then she admits, "Of course, you're going to want to end up with a doctor, because you'll have security for the rest of your life. But if it's a matter of, you know, then you've got to go with the firemen."

After filming the pilot, Margulies became a nurse on *ER*. The show also starred Ving Rhames, Mary Mara, Lee Tergesen, Adam Trese, and Onifaida Lampley. The TV movie Engine 50 was a 1993 Seagrave, which ultimately was assigned to Philly's Engine 2. *Philly Heat* (working title: *"Philly Fire"*) was directed by John David Coles (*Northern Exposure, Sex in the City*), with music by Wendy Blackstone. Executive producer was Tom Fontana for

Reeves Entertainment. The pilot took a long time from script to airing, as the first script draft is dated November 1992. The pilot episode was titled "Light My Fire."

In March of 1996, *Firehouse* began filming in New York for CBS Television. Starring Richard Dean Anderson (*MacGyver*) as Lieutenant Michael Brooks on L-60, the show centered around the Station house of FDNY Engine 17, Ladder 60, "The Pride of the Lower East side" with Battalion 5. The pilot dealt with a sniper targeting firefighters, "because they can't shoot back," and the introduction of a female paramedic (Gia Carides as Charlotte Brooks) into the station house with the merger of the FDNY & EMS. The sixty-minute pilot, which was set to air as a 96/97 mid-season replacement did not air in the United States until 2001. The option for six additional episodes was never completed. Richard Dean Anderson now stars in the cable Showtime series *Stargate SG-1* (also produced by Anderson for Gekko Film Corp), so it was doubtful if they ever will, as the Sci-Fi Channel had signed Anderson for its seventh season of Stargate SG-1.

In December 1997, a somewhat disjointed version, reedited to a ninety-minute movie with female nudity, and in which Anderson (as Lt. Brooks) is killed by the sniper, aired in Great Britain, and later throughout Europe and Australia. Its first US airing, edited to remove the nudity, was five years later in March 2001 on cable's TNN. The movie also starred Emmy award winner Edie Falco (*Oz, The Sopranos*). Originally titled *Engine 24 -Ladder 3*, the promo states "New York City, nine million inhabitants all live in constant threat of one of life's worst nightmares - fire. The only thing that protects this overcrowded metropolis from burning is Engine Company 24's crew of firefighters."

The engine and truck used in the movie were new 1996 Seagrave apparatus, and were returned to the Seagrave Company after shooting for use as demo models. Eventually, they both made it back to

New York; the Engine going to the Bureau of Training, and the Ladder, an FWD/Seagrave Aerialscope Tower Ladder became L-77 by 1998. In actuality E-17 is a disbanded Engine (January 1991), and L-60, is a fictional Ladder Co. The original working title unit numbers are in fact in-service Engine & Ladder Co. numbers for the FDNY, but are not housed together. The firehouse used was the old headquarters of Engine 17 and Ladder 18, at 185 Broome St. in Manhattan.

Rysher Entertainment produced *Firehouse,* in association with Fatima Productions and the Gekko Film Corporation, which Anderson runs with a partner. Technical advisor was Tim Brown FDNY, also one of the firefighter extras at the station. Brown, formerly with Rescue 3, has been detailed to New York's Office of Emergency Management (OEM) since 1999. The other "real" firefighters in the station are FDNY's Lt. Joe Brosi, currently a NYC Fire Marshal working back up in the Bronx; David Dangerfield of Squad 270; Ray Grawin who is retired from Rescue 3; Sam Melisi is now in Rescue Co 2, along with Pete Romeo. Don Schneider is a Lieutenant in Squad 252, and Phil Scozzarella is at Engine Co 73 in the South Bronx.

Phil Scozzarella also has a principal role in HBO's *Oz* as Correction Officer Joe Mineo, and Tim Brown portrays Correction Officer Jason Armstrong on the same show. Tim Brown, along with Lt. Chuck Margiotta, worked as firefighter extras on the movie *Frequency.* Margiotta, Dennis Quaid's Ladder Co. chauffer in the movie, lost his life September 11th in the WTC disaster. The series was created and written by Tom Fontana, who also Executive Produced. *Firehouse* can be found in some European video rental stores (in PAL format), and on Video CD. *Firehouse* aired as *Atesle Oyun* in Turkey.

L.A Firefighters starring Christine Else (*ER, BH 90210, Baywatch*) aired Sundays at 7:00pm, June 3 through July 8, 1996 on Fox for a summer run, before joining the fall lineup. The six episodes were shown airing against *60 Minutes* and *Dateline*. Assisted by LACoFD Capt. Steve Valenzuela, LACo PIO, as Technical Advisor, the show utilized the insignia and uniforms of the LA County Fire Department. The featured engine was a new KME Fire Apparatus, as Engine 132, provided to the show by KME. The truck (Truck 132) was an older ALF tillered aerial. Additional equipment responding out of the three-bay station is a HumVee, a Paramedic Squad unit, and a Battalion Chief. Apparatus drivers had no story involvement; the medics were rarely utilized on medical incidents, and were all but absent in the firehouse, and once the equipment arrives on the scene. Fire station location shots mainly utilized 'old' LA City Station 27, at 1355 N. Cahuenga Blvd. in Hollywood (a couple blocks SW of Sunset and Vine).

L.A. Firefighters Clockwise from the left: Brian Leckner as J.B. Baker, Alesandra Hedison as Kay Rizzo, Michael Gallagher as Lenny Rose, Christine Elise as Erin Coffey, Jarrod Emick as Jack Malloy, and Carlton Wilborn as Ray Grimes.
Fox Broadcasting Co. photo

While casting the pilot, the office was in a trailer on the Fox lot. It was parked next to the *NYPD Blue* street set (and you thought it was shot in New York), and Jimmy Smits, Dennis Franz, et al would be outside the area waiting to start a scene. After the pilot was cast, the producers rented a building that had been used for airplane parts manufacturing, next to the Van Nuys Airport, where they had production and casting offices on the second floor, and the sound stages on the first floor. There were buildings next to it made from metal that were used as fire sets. This was reportedly fun for the cast as they could go downstairs and watch them shoot the fire scenes. The producers then bought a building, an old military weapons plant in the San Fernando Valley, for shooting interior scenes. They also bought a building in Canoga Park, which is now Ray-Art Studios. It is a mini-studio where *Charmed* and *Dr. Laura* are also shot.

The show's creator, Executive Producer, and Head writer was Gordon Greisman. Some critics of the program labeled it "*Baywatch* in the Firehouse"; other critics were not so kind. Greisman publicly acknowledged that the show, which had some firefighters calling for a sponsor boycott, was not perfect. "We are learning, and with each succeeding episode we are striving to be more dramatically honest and accurate," Greisman said. He was reacting to complaints from an L.A. firefighters union official that the series depicted those in the profession as "dangerous, immoral, unprofessional malcontents." Elizabeth Mitchell (*Frequency*) had a small role in *L.A Firefighters* as wife of the station Captain. "It was terrible, wasn't it?" she says with unusual honesty of the fire show, "And I did *LA Firefighters* 'cause I had never been on TV before." (Recently, she has been in several episodes of ER).

In the fall, a revamp of *LA Firefighters* was aired. It had a new title, **Fire Co. 132**, and a new Executive Producer, Patrick Hasburgh, (*The A-team, Aspen Extreme, 21 Jump Street*), who also wrote episode seven. He and Greisman gave the show a new look, and attempted to address the concerns that the show was not realistic enough. Additionally, some characters were changed or eliminated, and three new characters added, a nurse, a firefighter, and a chopper pilot.

They were given a new department name; "Metro Fire," and the firefighters also became paramedics. A Bell 412 Helicopter had been added to the station roster of equipment as "Air Squad 132," and a new 1996 Pierce Quantum pumper replaced the KME. The Quantum was a demo model provided by Pierce Mfg. Thirteen episodes were ordered for the fall lineup set to air November 10 at 9:00pm. However, only seven were completed before production was shut down. Fox's new Entertainment Director, Peter Roth, ultimately doused it, and the seven new episodes have never aired in the US. The seven episodes were sold overseas in 1997, and still airs in syndication in several countries, although not in the US. "Fire Co. 132" lettering stayed on the out-of- service LA City station 27 for several months after shooting in the hopes of continued episodes. *TV Guide* ran an article on LA Firefighters in the June 1-7, 1996 issue.

The new firefighter in the retooled series was Alexandra Paul, (*Baywatch*) as T.K. Martin, the youngest firefighter in the crew. Alexandra, an actual EMT, joined the cast during September's filming due to a cast member injury. Alexandra Paul's twin sister, Caroline, a firefighter since 1989 with the San Francisco FD, wrote an autobiography entitled *Fighting Fire*, released in 1998, which has been nominated for a Pulitzer Prize, and negotiations are underway to develop it into a movie. The book is an account of her experience of being one of the first sixteen women in a 1400-person fire department to join the SFFD. As of 2001, there are 150 women in the department. She entered the academy for a SF radio station story about discrimination within the

SFFD, graduated, and is still a firefighter with the FD, giving up her journalism career.

Alexandra states thus: "Caroline was the one to whom I turned when I was offered *Fire Co. 132*. I did not get to do any ride-alongs because I was cast only a week before shooting began. Luckily I had read a lot of Caroline's writings about firehouse life, and I also got a crash course from her. Initially, I was only brought in as a recurring character, because one of the lead actresses had injured her foot. I had never seen the show, but Caroline had and hated it. She felt it was very unrealistic, especially in the portrayal of women as firefighters, with too much cleavage, and soap opera-type love affairs going on. All the firefighters she knew thought it was a disgrace to the profession, so she didn't want me to do the show unless it was radically changed, which Fox promised it was going to do, and actually, when she saw the seven episodes we did shoot, she thought it was a very good show." Alexandra goes on to say, "I admire firefighters very much, with my sister, Caroline, and my brother, Jonathan, both topping the list."

In early October 1996, Denver Pyle (a western character actor) read for a proposed TV series titled ***Firehouse 421***. It is unknown which network or studio was producing it, or if a pilot was ever filmed.

In late March and early April of 1997, a pilot titled ***The 119*** (911 backwards) was filmed utilizing the new LA City Fire Station 112, located at 444 S. Harbor Boulevard, Berth 86, Ports O' Call for exterior and interior shots. "119" is a fictitious Los Angeles City station number. The show was written by Gregory Widen, a former Orange County California firefighter/paramedic (for three years in the early 1980's) while studying screenwriting at UCLA, who was also the Supervising Producer. Widen also wrote the screenplay for the 1991 blockbuster movie *Backdraft*.

The 2-hour pilot, produced for CBS and Paramount Television, cost a reported six million dollars. It starred Gary Cole as Fire Investigator James Clevenger (Mike Brady in *A Very Brady Sequel*); Kathryn Harrold as Fire Investigator Katherine Larsen (*Chicago Hope*); Peter Onorati as Captain Sheppard (*Firehouse,* a 1987 sexual comedy (and Julia Roberts' first movie role-), *NYPD Blue, Walker, Texas Ranger*); Ingo Neuhaus (*ER, Jag, CSI*) as Monk, and Kyle Colerider-Krugh as James "Inky" Perry, the arsonist. Paulette Poliniski (Pauly P) portrayed Firefighter Mary Ryan, only on the job a year, and a Battalion Chief's granddaughter, and whose father, an LA City Captain, recently died during a second alarm fire. Kevin Tighe (*Emergency!*) appears in a cameo role as Battalion Chief Kieran Ryan, Mary's grandfather. Six "real" firefighters (extras) were active, volunteer, or retired firefighters from the area, and rounded out the cast, credited as "Burley 119ers."

The 119 script, a short sixty pages (some hour-long program scripts are around fifty pages) was filmed on a 17-day shooting schedule. The pilot is unaired as Paramount said it would never air, coming so hot on the heels of L.A Firefighters. It took CBS five years to air their previous firefighting pilot, Richard Dean Anderson's 1996 *Firehouse* on cable, so hopefully we will be able to see *The 119* soon.

The primary engines used were an open-cab Crown pumper, and an ALF tiller rented from Fire Protection Specialists, a cinema vehicle rental company. Others were from nearby Santa Fe Springs FD. In the movie there was a scene where the Crown was wrecked, being struck by a concrete truck. As with many actors that have stand-ins, so did the Crown. They didn't actually let them smash the engine, but had another Crown, which was "much less lovely," according to the rental company. It was painted to match, and modified by reducing its structural integrity with several well-placed cuts in the frame to make it crumple during the accident, in which firefighter Monk (Ingo Neuhaus) is killed.

TV Firefighters

Open cab Crown used in *The 119* pilot as well as *Rescue 77* and *St. Michael's Crossing*. Photo by Cinema Vehicle Services, North Hollywood.

Alf Tiller truck used in *The 119* pilot as well as *LA Firefighters*, *St. Michael's Crossing* and *Rescue 77*. Sold to Deamworks, Inc. for a feature titled "Evolution." Photo by Cinema Vehicle Services, North Hollywood

The show was directed by Robert Iscove (*Dark Angel, Firestarter 2: Rekindled*), and produced by John B. Moranville (*MacGyver*). Executive producer was Christopher Crowe (*H.E.L.P., Miami Vice*). To ensure authenticity the producers hired LAFD Captain Jim Featherstone as the Technical Advisor. "It was a very noble effort by Paramount to realistically depict our work," states Featherstone. "It was my understanding that *The 119* was the most expensive pilot ever shot by them. In film, "fire" will always be a tough antagonist to portray. The audience can't "feel" or "get into" the psyche of "the beast." If you remember, the makers of *Backdraft* had to "humanize" the fire."

"It was a very busy effects show," according to Greg C. Jensen Sr., Special Effects coordinator who also worked on *Emergency!* and *Sierra*. "I remember that the entire shooting crew was tested and fitted with breathing apparatuses, and were inside a fire stage while we used real smoke. Most shoots use safer white smoke. The producers got some very unexpected and good production value on the show. The look was so real. Well, I guess it was real," states Jensen. "We created a real fire atmosphere for the camera crews to shoot in. On *Emergency!* and other fire shows the smoke, when people were around, was always white, always. Black or colored smokes were used only in the exterior, where no one would be breathing the smoke, for it is very toxic."

"On this show we used black and gray composition smokes, a technical pyrotechnic formula, and very toxic. We also used fifty-five gallon drums to burn cardboard (similar to what was done in Widen's movie *Backdraft*), that were cut out on the bottom, so as to let air and a breeze in. We then pumped air into the bottom of the barrel and voilá, hot red sparks were everywhere on the set. The sparks could then be sent to the shooting area of the set with E-fans or Ritter fans (large 7' dia. 8 propped electric fans). Now add the flames, the black smoke, the burning debris in the air, and the actors. You have one exciting show," states Jensen.

For the program, Station 119 housed a pumper, Tiller, Search & Rescue unit, Boat 2 (the 17,000 GPM capacity "Ralph J. Scott"), helicopter, the offices of the arson unit, and Grendel, a 250-pound dog. In actuality Station 112 houses the Ralph J. Scott, a Rescue Ambulance, and two land-based apparatus. The Ralph J. Scott, named after a former LA City Fire Chief, was built in 1925, and is listed on the National Register of Historic Places, and designated a National Historic Landmark and is still in service.

Similarities between Widen's *Backdraft* and *The 119*; there was a Firefighter Nightingale in both projects. Fire Investigator

Clevenger *(The 119)* could have been Robert De Niro's brother *(Backdraft* Arson Investigator Rimgale), as they both talk to the fire and treat it like a living, breathing thing.

Similarities between 1981's *Code Red* starring Lorne Green and *The 119*; both are based in an LA City FD boathouse with a helicopter. Both have a new female recruit, arson teams quartered in the stations, a dog mascot that rides along on alarms, and both indicate a family of firefighters.

A bit of "119" trivia: In an October 1997 episode of *Diagnosis Murder*, "Malibu Fire," Randolph Mantooth portrays the Mayor and volunteer firefighter of a small community near Malibu threatened by fire. Most of the exteriors were shot at the famous "Rock Store," northwest of Malibu on Mullholland Highway. It is a favorite biker hangout that includes Jay Leno. Out on the fire line, Mantooth, as well as Dr. Sloan's policeman son – also a volunteer firefighter, is wearing fire gear with helmets from Station 119.

Emergency! trivia: In "Malibu Fire" there is an LA County GMC four-door Rescue unit with a large "51" on the side and "Rescue 51" on the rear. Other *Emergency!* actors, Robert Fuller, along with Jennifer Tighe (as a TV news reporter), who is the daughter of their former co-star Kevin Tighe appear in this episode, directed by *Emergency!* alumni Christian I. Nyby II. Actual fire footage from the devastating fire of 1993, which destroyed hundreds of homes in Malibu was utilized.

Family Brood was an unaired pilot centering around four generations of Irish-American FDNY firefighters in the O'Shea family. Starring Brian Cox (*Rob Roy, Braveheart*) as the patriarchal head of the family, Marin Hinkle (*Another World*), Dylan Bruno (*Carrie 2*), Patti Lupone (*Falcone*), Jessica Hecht (*Single Guy, Friends*) and Tony Award nominee Amy Ryan (*The Naked Truth*). Produced in 1998 for CBS by Rysher Entertainment, by Emmy award-winning writer and producer, Tom Fontana (*St. Elsewhere, Homicide, Oz*), with James Yoshimura (*Homicide*), and Barry Levinson (*Homicide, Oz*). Theme music was by Rusty Magee.

As for firefighters, Fontana states that he has hung out with them since childhood, when he lived half a block from a firehouse. "I know these guys. I drink with these guys. They're great people - the true heroes." Fontana has written two other pilots about firefighters, neither of which made it into series format, ABC's *Philly Heat*, with Peter Boyle, and CBS's *Firehouse*, starring Richard Dean Anderson.

St. Michael's Crossing was fimed throughout the Los Angeles and San Fernando Valley in March, 1999. Originally titled St. Elmo's Fire, it is labeled as a fire-rescue action/drama. Produced for CBS, this sixty-minute proposed pilot takes place in an LA station housing police, firefighters, and paramedics, who respond together as a special task force. The station utilized was LA City's old Station 27. It starred Michael Chiklis (*The Commish, The Shield*), Beau Starr (*Due South*), Geoffrey Gould, as the Detective, Harry J Lennix (*Ally McBeal*), Kevin Dillon (*That's Life*), Justin Louis (*Fighting Fitzgerald's*), Lauren Vélez (*Oz*), and Allison Smith (*Buddy Faro, The West Wing*). Co-producer was Dennis Murphy (*Magnificent 7, Buffy the Vampire Slayer*) for Regency Entertainment, Badlands Entertainment, and CBS Productions. Head writer and co-producer was Jorge Zamacona (*ER, NYPD Blue, Homicide, Third Watch*).

Robert Butler directed the pilot. If picked up, the series was to air on Saturday nights, and is reminiscent of 1990's *H.E.L.P.* The pilot was being filmed about the same time as *Third Watch*, although on the opposite coast, and apparently never made it through production. According to Jorge Zamacona's representative at the Creative Artist Agency, filming was not completed or at least finished editing, and so will never air. St. Michael is the patron and protector of police officers, EMT's, and paramedics – so who was protecting the firefighters? New apparatus was not utilized, as Cinema Vehicle Services of North Hollywood provided fire apparatus. Most likely the Crown was from *The 119*, and the ALF tillered aerial from *LA Firefighters*, and *The 119*, recently purchased from Fire Protection Specialists. Cinema Vehicle Services currently provides fire and ambulance equipment for *CSI, CSI: Miami, Crossing Jordan, Boomtown*, and others.

Michael Chiklis currently stars in Fox Television's *Rampart* (since retitled). No, not a story about the hospital from *Emergency!* but about a rogue police detective loosely based on LA City's real Rampart Division of the LAPD. The one-hour weekly series, created by writer-producer Shawn Ryan (*Nash Bridges*), who will executive-produce the series with Scott Brazil (*L.A. Doctors, Hill Street Blues*). No surprise that the department is ticked off about the title. Sgt. John Pasquariello, an LAPD spokesman, told the LA Times, "Shows like these capitalize on sensational headlines without realizing what harm that can do." The hour-long weekly series began as a mid-season replacement on March 12, 2002. Thirteen episodes of Rampart were ordered. Due to the negative press by the LAPD over the series name, it has been renamed *The Shield*. Still set in Los Angeles, and still controversial, it has been renewed for Fall 2002/03. So it looks like *St. Michaels's Crossing* is not going to air.

A drama by Aaron Spelling (Spelling Television) for the Warner Brothers Network (originally proposed to ABC) is titled **Rescue 77**. The original title for the pilot and series was *Rescue 8*. In the February 1998 issue of *Variety Magazine*, a Warner Brothers release states, "*Rescue 8* is about emergency paramedics from Spelling in the fall lineup." In fact, it would not be until a year later, in March 1999 that the series would air as *Rescue 77*.

Rescue 77 focused on three L.A. firefighter/paramedics, who only had minor interaction with the rest of Station 77's "C" Shift crew

Rescue 77 cast
L-R: Victor Brown as Michael Bell, Richard Roundtree as Captain Durfee, Christian Kane as Wick Lobo, and Marjorie Monaghan as Kathleen Ryan.
Photo by Richard Cartwright

of the Engine and Truck. Technically neither LA City nor County, they operate as the Los Angeles Fire Authority, and are "first on the scene of disaster, and the last hope of the critically injured." The sixty-minute series aired March 15 through May 3, 1999. Thirteen episodes were ordered but only eight were completed before production was shut down. Gregory Widen, (*Backdraft, The 119, Highlander*) created the series for Spelling, wrote the pilot episode, completed in early March 1998 as *Rescue 8*, and was its Executive Producer. All references to Engine 8, Station 8 etc. in the script were, of course, later changed to "77."

Returning as a firefighter and senior medic on the shortened series was Marjorie Monaghan, who portrayed a New York City firefighter in the 1990 series *H.E.L.P.* Her appearance in *H.E.L.P.* was her first television series. In addition to the title change, Monaghan's character name was also changed from Allison Harris to Kathleen Ryan during the pilot rewrite. The Captain in charge of the unit was Richard Roundtree, in his second appearance as a TV firefighter (see *Firehouse*, 1973). "I thought I had an appreciation (for firefighting) prior to doing this, but learning who and what a Captain does, what firemen actually do from day to day, and what the rescue paramedics do, is mind boggling," says Roundtree.

Technical assistance by LA City was withdrawn after a script review

Richard Roundtree as Captain Durfee in *Rescue 77*
Photo by Richard Cartwright

Marjorie Monaghan as Kathleen Ryan in *Rescue 77*
Photo by Richard Cartwright

of the proposed pilot. An LA County Fire Department advisor was brought on board, and assisted with a revamped pilot and subsequent episodes. The series TA even appeared in a few of the episodes. Uniforms and fire gear were patterned after those worn by LA City. Firefighter extras were a mix of LA County and City, as well as other local firefighters throughout the area. John

Sarvis was the aerial coordinator for the series. His piloting of helicopters for movies and TV (*Code 3*, *CHiPs*, *The 119*) include almost fifty other films and TV programs.

Fire Station 77's location was filmed in the City of Glendale, Northeast of Los Angeles, at an earthquake-damaged, unused fire station scheduled for demolition. Former Station 21, is located at 210 S. Orange Street, and can be seen in a circa 1926 photograph at http://fire.ci.glendale.ca.us/history/sta21p37.html. Exterior shots of the paramedic base station hospital, known as "City Hospital" were filmed at Woodruff Community Hospital in Long Beach at 3800 Woodruff Avenue, west of the I-605. Don't go looking for the "Firefighters Bar," as it only existed on the studio back lot. LA City Station 27 was used as the home base of a "rival" group of firefighters (as Station 27), who used to harass the *Rescue 77* firefighters and paramedics with horseplay and practical jokes. They showed the station exterior when the *Rescue 77* crew went over to pay that group back with a practical joke of their own.

The fire apparatus featured on Rescue 77 was a new Pierce Saber pumper, and a Freightliner/American LaFrance truck. An older open-cab Crown Engine (used in *The 119*) was used occasionally,

Engine, ambulance, and ALF tiller parked on Plainview Avenue in front of Verdugo Hills High School for the filming of an episode of *Rescue 77*.

and the crew would swap from the Pierce to the Crown for no apparent reason, in the same episode, as the two engines are never in the station simultaneously. The same can be said of the truck; they swapped from the ALF/LTI turntable ladder, to an ALF tillered aerial (also used in *LA Firefighters* and *The 119*) in the same episode. There was never any explanation for this swapping of apparatus.

Freightliner/Wheeled Coach provided two different Rescue Ambulance units on Ford E-450 Super-Duty chassis. The second RA used in the program, by Wheeled Coach, was in their "FireMedic" series, whose interior was large enough to be specially outfitted for camera mounting. This RA (currently owned by Cinema Vehicle Services) was recently seen in Arnold Schwarzenegger's *"Collateral Damage"* (2002). Unable to always get the same fire/rescue HumVee for the series, it would either be fully equipped, or have a basic (empty) pick-up style bed. *Rescue 77* never made it out of the 90's overall share rating, out of 1 to 100 rated programs. *Rescue 77* aired as *Pelastus 77* in Finland

An unaired firefighting pilot titled **Firehouse One** was shot in LA City in the summer of 1999, utilizing 'old' LA City Fire Station 46. A FOX-Television production starring StevenWilliams (*X-Files* (Mr. X), *Firetrap*, as a Fire Chief), which was a situation comedy set in a fire station with a cast of misfit firefighters that included comedians Jeff Mayse and Joby Saad as firefighters. An off duty LA County Firefighter, Brent Burton, was hired to drive the apparatus, and had a short cameo role in the opening credits. Other extras were students from the James Shern Fire Academy in Compton, California. The show was written and produced for Sony Pictures by Jim Vickers, who is mainly credited as a movie stunt-coordinator (*Mask of Zorro, Ace Ventura*). Elayne Keratsis (*Peter Benchley's Creatures, Bodyguard*) directed the pilot. No specific city or fire department was inferred. The engine used was a retired LAFD 1970 Seagrave.

Billy Blazes, Sam Sparks, and Wendy Waters are three firefighting members of an elite ten-member rescue squad called *Rescue Heroes*: Global Response Team. With their combined skills of firefighting, police work, and other special talents, they answer the call for help around the world. This animated feature series began airing October 1999 on CBS, and is based on the Fisher-Price® preschool action figures, modeled on non-violent, real-life heroes. There are currently thirteen thirty-minute episodes in the series, which airs at 8:00am on Saturdays. CBS Television, Nelvana Productions in Canada, and Teletoon in China produces the show. Videos, action figures, rescue gear, vehicles, and toothbrushes are available at most toy stores.

On November 1, 2001 a limited edition of Billy Blazes dressed in New York fire gear featuring FDNY logos was released to honor the New York Firefighters. It was made available only in the New York area at Toys-R-Us stores. Initially conceived in 2000 with a run of 30,000 units with only a portion of the retail price of $9.99 to go towards the FDNY Fire Safety Education Fund. However since the tragic events of September 11, 2001, the entire amount will be donated to benefit the Education Fund with the edition run increased to 105,000 units. The toys are "selling out as quickly as they're hitting shelves," according to Neil Friedman, president and chief executive of Fisher-Price, "If all the figures sell, the fund will make more than $ 1 million dollars". FDNY's Billy Blazes quickly sold out of course and on the secondary market was fetching over $60.00 on the internet auction site eBay. Other characters with FDNY logos are firefighters Manny Hattan and Wendy Waters along with Matt Medic an EMT. Other non-FDNY characters are Ben Choppin, a forest ranger, and Aidan Assist, an EMT. In 2001, Billy Blazes was voted "Toy of the Year" in the 'Infant and Preschool' category. A Rescue Heroes metal die-cast 5-pac was released in 2002 featuring Billy Blazes on the side of the Fire Truck.

CHAPTER SIX — THIRD WATCH

Third Watch, co-created by Emmy award-winner John Wells (*ER, The West Wing*), previewed on NBC on September 23rd 1999, in the US and Canada, with over 20 million viewers in the U.S. tuning in, ranking it the fourth highest Nielsen-rated show for the week. *Third Watch* is primarily a Police/EMS drama, with a smidgen of fire thrown in. This medical-emergency program is often called "ER on wheels."

The term *Third Watch* is a misnomer as it is actually called "Tour 3" in NYC, referring to the 4:00pm to midnight shift (3:00pm to 11:00pm in the series). It is meaningful only to the PD and EMS as the FDNY run two shifts - 9:00am - 6:00pm (Day Tour) and

Season One cast of *Third Watch*
NBC Photo by Chris Haston

6:00pm to 9:00am (Night Tour). However, in the program, the FD, PD, and EMS all end their shifts at 11:00pm to remain constant with the program's title. The series, which began shooting in July 1999, on location in New York City, Queens, the Bronx, and Brooklyn, chronicles two teams of FDNY-EMS paramedic units, 55-2 and 55-3, and two police units of the 55th Precinct, 55-Charlie and 55-David.

Rounding out the nine-member cast is firefighter Jimmy Doherty at Fire Station 55, who in the first season responded on Engine Co. 57, or Ladder 100, as the scene dictated. This "super" firefighter is always on the nozzle, makes all the rescues, operates all the extrication equipment, uses the radio (instead of the Captain) to request additional equipment or resources, and seemingly only takes his orders from the Battalion Chief. He is also the non alimony-paying ex-husband of one of the medics, Kim, on unit 55-2. The rest of the fire crew is listed as guest stars in the credits; many are off-duty NY firefighters. Two routinely featured members of Engine 57 are real NY firefighters, Bill Walsh as "Walsh" and Derek Kelley as "DK."

The first season's Engine Company 57's responsibilities have been taken over by FDNY's Special Operations Unit, beginning with season two with Squad 55. A Squad is a freelance engine that responds to all working alarms in its district. The Squad number now corresponds with the house number, and is now referred to as Squad 55, as opposed to Station 55. However, the canopy in front of the station still says Engine Co. 57 – Ladder 100. On large incidents we will still see E-57 / L-100, but with Jimmy Doherty on Squad 55. According to Eddie Cibrian, as firefighter Jimmy Doherty, there almost wasn't a fire aspect to this series. Cibrian says his character was slow to introduce, as he was a late member of the cast. Before he met with John Wells "There wasn't even a fireman in the show. I met with him, and we talked, and he decided to add a fireman character," states Cibrian.

Episode four in the second season adds a female firefighter to the crew of Squad 55, Amy Carlson, a 1998 Emmy nominee, as firefighter Alex Taylor. Alex was recently transferred from another station due to a sexual harassment suit, and is a former FDNY paramedic who still does occasional Medic overtime shifts with 55-2 and 55-3. The FDNY hired their first woman firefighter in September 1982, and currently have thirty-three women in fire suppression. Nine of these women are currently on leave pending retirement. The remaining twenty-four cover every rank from probationary firefighter, firefighter, chief's aids, fire marshal, lieutenants, and captain. There is one woman on the current promotion list to lieutenant, the two women lieutenants are on the current promotion list to captain, and captain is on the current promotion list to Battalion Chief.

Eddie Cibrian as firefighter
Jimmy Doherty
NBC Photo

Amy Carlson as firefighter/medic
Alex Taylor
NBC Photo

In a surprise move for the fans, Paramedic Bobby Caffey (Bobby Cannavale), Kim's partner on 55-2, was shot and killed midway through the second season (Episode 2:16). Cannavale complained to Wells that he was not getting enough to do, and that the producers were looking to pull in more female viewers by focusing more on the female characters. No miraculous TV recovery here as Cannavale asked to be written out and Wells obliged. As a result Alex Taylor is taken off Squad 55, and assigned to paramedic unit 55-2 in season three.

Third Watch is produced by John Wells Productions, in association with Warner Brothers Television, for two million dollars per episode, on a fourteen-hour day, ten-day shooting schedule. "On *Third Watch*, I'm very involved in the writing of the show and the editing and producing," states Wells. (The scripts are written in Los Angeles). "Because it's shot in New York the production is handled by Brooke Kennedy and my co-executive producer, Chris Chulack, a wonderful director who supervises the visual end of the show."

After airing only four episodes, NBC ordered a twenty-two episode commitment in its first season. Its original time slot of Sunday at 8:00pm was moved to Monday at 10:00pm in January 2000, airing against *Family Law* and *20/20*, where it attracted a larger audience base, and maintained a steady thirty overall rating, occasionally breaking into the twenties. In the second season, *Third Watch* switched focus from the action sequences of fires, explosions, and people trapped in buildings, to character-driven stories that spotlight each of the show's ten characters and their personal problems, both at work and at home. "Audiences felt there were too many characters," says Warner Bros. Television President, Peter Roth, (formerly President of Fox Entertainment Group, 1996-1999, who dumped *Fire Co. 132*). "We're going to be focusing a lot more on the characters' personal lives, and doing a little bit less rescuing," say Wells and Chulack.

With less "action" than the first season, the ratings dropped into the fifties, but by episode seven of the second season, the format reverted somewhat to season one's popular format, and the ratings climbed back into the high twenties. Season three (fall 2001) was rescheduled to begin an hour earlier at 9:00pm, although still on Mondays. The ratings drop to the thirties and forties, coming in last in its time slot. In Canada the program still airs at 10:00pm on CTV, and the show places consistently in the Top 20.

Notable guest stars have been Jack Klugman, Mia Farrow, Gerald McRaney, Rosie O'Donnell, Roy Scheider, and Sean Young. Three former cast members from the acclaimed police drama *Hill Street Blues* (NBC 1981-87) portray Alex Taylor's mother (Veronica Hammel), uncle (Bruce Weitz), and her father's best friend (Ed Marinaro) in the season three finale.

The paramedics and firefighters in the series are housed together in "Camelot Station," so nicknamed for its location at the corner of the fictitious King and Arthur Streets. (Arthur Avenue is up in the Bronx, and King Street is in Greenwich Village in Manhattan). In actuality there are 220 fire stations in the City of New York, and not one houses a paramedic unit. During the first season, it was incorrectly called Station 55 (which is an actual working single-bay station in Little Italy in Manhattan), with the 55th Police Precinct across the street. In the first season, fire station exteriors were shot at FDNY's E-258 / L-115 at 10-40 47th Ave. (136 8th Street), in Queens, formerly Long Island City.

The second season's firehouse exterior location shots moved to an unused firehouse near the corner of Broadway and Bedford, in the Williamsburg section of Brooklyn, and then to a station in the Northwest section of Brooklyn, in an area called Greenpoint. In episode ten (season two) the crew is outside yet another station, a single-bay firehouse. The first season's fire station was undergoing major renovations, including repair for fire damage sustained early

2000, hence all the scaffolding out in front. *Third Watch* was back using Engine 258/Ladder 115 station for exteriors in season three.

There is no police station across the street. In fact the closest one is the 108th Precinct, which is three blocks away on 50th Ave. The building utilized is an in-use building shot for exteriors only. There is no 55th Precinct in NYC.

During the first season, interiors of the firehouse, kitchen, dayroom, locker area (which doubled for the cops locker area), ER Triage area, police precinct etc. were filmed on a sound stage on the West side of Manhattan. New York's Bellevue Hospital, called "Angel of Mercy" was used during the first season for the hospital interior and exterior shots. For the second and subsequent seasons, sets moved to a studio (created out of a complete block of buildings renovated for the *Third Watch* production company), in the Greenpoint section of Brooklyn about a mile from Engine 258's fire station. New sets have been added, including the second floor bunkroom; police precinct, including the second floor, and now their own locker room, and hospital ER/Trauma floor. *Third Watch* uses Red Cross signage as part of their set design in the hospital (now called "Our Lady of Mercy" or sometimes simply referred to as "Mercy") waiting room, insurance areas, and their new Neo-Natal ICU.

On December 6, 2002, in true fashion of coincidence, more than a hundred firefighters and twenty-five pieces of equipment responded to a fire at 196 Diamond Street in Brooklyn at the Greenpoint, NY studios of NBC's *Third Watch*. The fire was quickly contained, but one firefighter suffered a minor injury, and a civilian was taken to Bellevue Hospital, where he was treated for smoke inhalation. "I guess they got a little taste of what their show is all about," said Chief Michael Rowley of Battalion 45. "There were no serious injuries, but there was extensive damage to the interior of the building." Chief Rowley also found some irony in the fire. "They shot exteriors for that show outside Engine Co. 258, and Engine 258 was among the first units to respond to the fire." The building houses the production offices, art department, and studio space for the show.

In the first season, featured fire equipment was a reserve 1997 Seagrave Fire Apparatus loaned to the show by the FDNY and repainted "57" (an unused FDNY number) for the program. (Engine 57 was located in Manhattan at the Battery, and was taken out of service in 1959). In the last few episodes of season one, they begin using an engine manufactured by E-1 as Engine 57. This E-1, a 1993, 1250 GPM "Hush" pumper (similar to the "Cyclone" series) was loaned to the show by E-1, painted to FDNY specs by NY City Shops, and the Seagrave went back into reserve. Prior to 9/11 there was one 1997 Seagrave used as a training Engine at Randall's Island, so possibly this is it. However, with all the shifting of apparatus after 9/11 I am not sure where it is today.

The engine from *Third Watch* is the only E-1 in service, so to speak, in NYC. It has been renumbered "55" for the second season, and sports a Tasmanian devil mascot on the front grill. (The FDNY had an E-1 in 1995, but only on a loan basis for evaluation). At the beginning of the third season, the crew gets a new E-1, but in actuality it's the same one with the Taz removed, and replaced by the US flag. In season four, the Taz is back. Also housed in the fire station is a Seagrave truck (first two seasons) as Ladder 100, a fictional Ladder

Emergency One aparatus as Squad 55
Photo by Movie Time Cars, New York

Company number (looks like an '84 or '85 Seagrave, probably reserve or spare fleet donated to the show by the department). Season three's Ladder is a 1991 Mack CF Tower Ladder. Battalion 24 is also a fictitious number.

In the series, the medic units are Horton Ambulances on Ford Econoline F-350's (and they really are called a "bus" in NYC). They park on the street, as there is no room in the fire station. The Medic Unit designations, A55-2 and B55-3, (sometimes referred to as A55-3) are fictitious, and are simply radio call signs to help the viewer identify them. To be correct for the program the two unit numbers should be "24P3" and "24S3," as the first number in the unit name is the Battalion they are based in or assigned to. The letter denotes the type of unit they are; A through M is for a Basic Life Support (BLS) rig and N through Z is for Advanced Life Support (ALS) ambulances. The last number is the tour number. (For real example: 8T3 Battalion 8 (Manhattan), ALS Bus, Tour 3). In the series they work in Battalion 24's area, and are ALS rigs and both work Tour 3 (or the Third Watch), hence 24P3 and 24S3. When being called on the radio it would be '24Paul' or '24Sam.' However, this would not be in keeping with the 55th Precinct and Fire Station 55 designations.

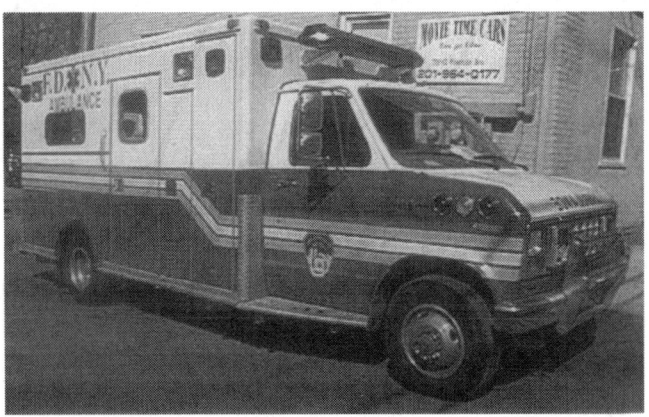

Ambulance used on *Third Watch* Photo by Movie Time Cars, New York

The Medic crews could be seen arriving on scene in the "wrong" unit designated ambulance in early episodes. Probably for this reason the medic unit numbers, 55-2 and 55-3, have been subsequently removed from their ambulance. In reality, medic units in NYC don't have their unit numbers on their rigs. The medics are not housed with fire suppression companies, but do have station assignments. They work eight-hour shifts, five days a week with two days off, repeat schedule, then three days off.

There are Technical Advisors (TA's) assigned for the hospital doctors, medics, and PD, and in the second season Battalion Chief Brian Dixon, from the FDNY Office of Public Information, was added as the Fire Department technical advisor. Brian serves as the liaison between the show's producers and the FDNY. He reviews the scripts and dailies, and makes suggestions. He also occasionally appears in the program as Dixon. Chief Dixon was one of only two Chief Officers, out of five, from his command location to survive the WTC collapse, who arrived just as the second plane hit.

John Hanchar, Paramedic Lieutenant assigned to FDNY's EMS Command, was the overall TA for the series during the first two seasons; he is currently a police officer for Rockland County, NY. Charlie Wells FDNY EMS Department Deputy Chief replaced Hanchar during season two as the Paramedic TA along with Paramedic Christine Mazzola. Other Technical Advisors are Officer Mike Keenan for the Police, and Alice Niederlander for the Hospital scenes with Mark Morocco as medical advisor.

John Wells states, "What I'm interested in with drama is something that illuminates the human condition in a way that we can better ourselves. We can watch someone else make mistakes that we think we ourselves would be able to make. We try to find those small moments of heroism and moral dilemmas; they're close to the same kinds of choices we all have to make day in and day out."

"Let's experience those emotions, try them on a little bit, and hopefully we can use that in our own lives. The three shows (*ER, The West Wing,* and *Third Watch*) have elements in common - the most visible being fast-paced, steadicam action. Whether it's emergency personnel racing along with patients on gurneys, presidential aides hurrying down corridors, or firefighters racing to a fire, all of these series have large casts with interlocking storylines," states Wells.

The first collectable, other than scripts and cast photos, is the December 4th 1999 issue of *TV Guide*, which has five cast members on the cover. This cover issue, in English and French, with a related article was released ONLY in Canada. There are other regional TV weekly-type magazines with one or more cast members on the cover, including those from Australia and the UK. *TV Guide,* again only in Canada, released a cover of three cast members with a related article on January 26, 2002. The show performs much better in the ratings in Canada than in the US in the 10pm time slot, which could explain why they have twice featured the show on the cover of *TV Guide*. *Third Watch* airs Tuesday evenings at 10pm in the UK on the Sky One Network, as well as various other days and times throughout Europe and Australia. The show debuted July 17, 2000 in New Zealand, and ran a cover feature story in the July 15-21, 2000, *NZ TV Guide*. The July 15-21, 2000 edition of *NZ TV Day Magazine* also featured two members of *Third Watch* on the cover. There are *Third Watch* items available at the Warner Brothers Studio Store. On occasion some items from end of season cast parties have shown up on eBay such as mugs, briefcases, jackets, and other items.

A&E Network has acquired *Third Watch* for an estimated $700,000 per episode from Warner Bros. A&E may choose to air the show up to five times a week for the full 8 years, provided of course NBC continues to renew the series on the network. *Third Watch* premiered on A&E September 1, 2002, and aired Monday through Thursday. Just before the last episode of season three aired, it was announced that *Third Watch* had been picked up for a fourth season.

Trivia: *Emergency!* buffs will rejoice at the name for the donut-fed (by the PD) Dalmatian in the firehouse, "Mantooth," in honor of the TV series *Emergency!* The Dalmatian belonged to the Paramedic that was shot in the opening episode, hospitalized, and then medically retired, taking the dog with him. Two of the cast members are no strangers to firefighting; Skipp "Sully" Sudduth, the veteran cop was a firefighter opposite Richard Dean Anderson in the 1996 pilot *Firehouse*. Michael "Doc" Beach starred in the TV movie *Fire! Trapped on the 37th Floor* with Lee Majors. Another bit of trivia/history is in season one, episode nine where *Third Watch* remembers the 1958 series *Rescue 8*. The rescue crews assisting Engine 57 and Ladder 100 in removing the large lady from her upper story apartment are wearing *Res8cue* logos on their jackets. There is no Rescue 8 unit in New York; this is the second time that the 1958 series has been 'remembered' in a TV fire series. Jimmy's badge number is 5669, (serial number 06171) and Amy's is 6302. Ironically, in France *Third Watch* is called "New York 911."

Usually its stars that crossover to other programs, but on November 21, 2001, a new episode of NBC's *Law and Order* (The fire this time), showed *Third Watch* FDNY Unit 55-3 ambulance at a fire scene. Unit number "55-3" appears in the upper rear left corner of the bus, just where it used to be in the first half of season one of *Third Watch*. Strangely enough though, the numbers "55-3" and "55-2" have not been seen on the rigs for two years. They panned too quickly to notice if the fire equipment was also from *Third Watch*.

In the April 1, 2002 episode the 'real' Ladder 115 was sitting outside the station (inside joke?), as they film at Engine 258 / Ladder 115. In episode four of season four from out of the past comes Engine 17 assisting Squad 55. E-17 was last seen in Richard Dean Anderson's *Firehouse* pilot in 1996.

In the April 25, 2002 episode of *ER*, a family emergency summons Dr. Lewis (Sherry Stringfield) to New York, where she works with *Third Watch* cops Molly Price and Jason Wiles, and paramedics Kim Raver and Amy Carlson. Lewis' storyline concludes on the April 29 episode of *Third Watch*. This episode ranked an unprecedented thirteenth in the Nielsen Ratings, becoming the first time it has broken into the teens since the series began. With an adjusted season three start, there are twenty-one original aired drama episodes, plus the two-hour season opening special.

Perhaps it's due to there being more awards shows than ever before, but *Third Watch* has garnered more nominations and awards than any other fire/rescue/EMS program. The following are nominations and awards won for the *Third Watch* actors and crew:

Third Watch was nominated for "Favorite New Dramatic Series" in the *26th Annual People's Choice Awards* held on January 9th, 2000. Michael Beach was nominated for "Outstanding Actor in a Drama Series" for *Third Watch* in the February 2000 *Image Awards*. The TV Guide Awards held in March listed for consideration *Third Watch* as "Favorite New Series," and "Favorite Actor in a New Series" for both Michael Beach and Eddie Cibrian. John Wells received the Vision Award in the television category given by the Producers Guild of America at the March 2000 *PGA Golden Laurel Awards* ceremony.

The Motion Pictures Sound Editors, USA, nominated *Third Watch* for the Golden Reel award for "Best Sound Editing" for the pilot episode, *Welcome to Camelot*. Both Bobby Cannavale and Eddie Cibrian were nominated for "Best Emerging Actor in a Drama Series" by the American Latino Media Arts (ALMA), formerly known as the Bravo Awards, in its fifth Annual ceremony. *Third Watch* won twelve Emmy's in the 52nd Annual awards program held in September 2000, all in the "Outstanding Sound Editing For A Series" category for the pilot *Welcome to Camelot*. (The 12

Emmy recipients in this category were for sound, dialogue, foley, ADR, and music).

On May 31st 2001, *Third Watch* was awarded the American Women in Radio & Television's Gracie Allen Award for Outstanding National Entertainment Program-Drama. The "Gracies" encourage the positive portrayal of women in entertainment. During its fifth Annual ceremony, *Third Watch* received the Prism Award for the episodes *Know Thy Self* and *After Hours*. Prism recognizes work in which members of the entertainment community take an active roll addressing drug abuse in America. *Third Watch* was nominated for an Imagen Award for "Best TV Drama." The 16th Annual Imagen Awards honor positive portrayals of Latinos, and were presented on June 14th, 2001. At the 53rd Annual Emmy awards presentation, in November 2001, *Third Watch* was nominated for "Sound Editing for a Series" for *Honor*, an episode depicting the devastating warehouse fire where three firefighters from a rival company lose their lives.

At the *61st Annual George Foster Peabody Awards*, announced March 27, 2002, *Third Watch* received the Broadcast Excellence award for the episode *In Their Own Words*, a special episode providing an occasion for the New York police, fire, and medical professionals to recount their personal experiences of 9/11. It was the only Network drama series honored. The *Third Watch* episode Requiem for a Bantamweight (episode 2:15) has received a nomination for a *Prism Award*, which honor the accurate portrayal of drug and alcohol use, and addiction in the entertainment industry.

The awards are presented by the Entertainment Industry Council, a nonprofit group that encourages social responsibility in the entertainment world, along with the Robert Wood Johnson Foundation, and the National Institute on Drug Abuse. The ceremony took place May 9, 2002. Eddie Cibrian was nominated for an ALMA Award at its sixth annual ceremony in May 2002 as "Outstanding Actor in a Television Series," and Jesús Treviño was nominated as "Outstanding Director of a Television Drama or Comedy" for the episode *Adam 55-3*. The ALMA Awards are presented by the National Council of La Raza, and honor achievements by Latinos in the entertainment industry. *Third Watch* was nominated for "Outstanding Sound Editing" for *Falling*, and "Outstanding Stunt Coordination" for *Superheroes*, at the September 22, 2002 Emmy Awards.

Third Watch Starts and Ends Its Third Season On a Somber Note

One result of the terrorist attack in New York on September 11, 2001, although obviously minor in nature in comparison, was that the filming of *Third Watch* was shutdown. Water and all the portable generators utilized on the set were given to the search and rescue effort, and lighting technicians and other crewmembers donated their services. Brooke Kennedy, who also serves as one of the show's executive producers, organized relief efforts, catering facilities at the show's Brooklyn studios were revved up, and hot food was prepared and distributed to rescue workers. Lights used for night shooting were loaned to rescue teams. A reservoir of medical and fire supplies used during shooting were donated to the city. Television production resumed on the 27th for an episode shooting in Harlem.

When the producers of *Third Watch* decided to provide a forum for New York rescue workers to tell their 9/11 stories, they worried about appearing exploitative. But John Wells, executive producer, said it quickly became clear that firefighters, police officers, and paramedics welcomed the chance to talk. Wells conducted most of the interviews during the two-hour unscripted tribute, which featured the cast interacting with real New York firefighters, policemen, and paramedics, who gave their personal accounts of 9/11.

Cast members introduced the unscripted segments thus: "We had people who worked for us who are no longer alive. We were searching for an appropriate way to come back. This will be a tribute to all the people; it will be their stories." I asked three questions and somebody would speak for 45 minutes," Wells stated. "These are people who want to tell their stories, and who want to make sure their stories are heard. They had a kind of courage and dedication that I'm not sure I could ever possess," he said.

Actors in the series sat in on the interview sessions and will be seen in the special. While shooting was underway at one station house, Wells recalled, some of the firefighters' wives showed up. Out of respect, he was going to call off the interviews, but found the spouses were eager to be heard. Molly Price, who plays policewoman Faith Yokas on *Third Watch*, was also interviewed on the program. She is married to FDNY firefighter Derek Kelly, who survived and participated in the rescue operation, and has a recurring role in *Third Watch* as firefighter DK.

Some of the safety and rescue workers in the special are a regular part of *Third Watch*, serving either as consultants or actors. "They're closely associated with people in the emergency rescue field, and lost many of their technical advisors," says Patricia Reed Scott, commissioner of the Mayor's Office of Film, Theater, and Broadcasting. The "real people" associated with the series helped give it authenticity, and many of them, Wells says, "Participated in the rescue operation, and were there at the time of the evacuation, and the collapse of the towers. We had people who worked for us who are no longer alive." In an interview with *TV Guide*, Jason Wiles (Bosco) states, "It was really important for us to do the tribute. We're in New York, so we couldn't just go on with the show. We lost thirteen rescue workers who worked second jobs on the show as extras."

When Amy Carlson stood on the rooftop of her building, and watched the World Trade Center crumble on Sept. 11, all she could think of were the firefighters. "I knew they were inside," she says. Unfortunately, she later found out that she was right. "There was no way to portray the FDNY without incorporating this [the tragedy] into the fabric of who they are," said Carlson. "And it will never be the same for them." T. Sean Ferguson, a first assistant director, said, "Three police officers and six firefighters who worked on *Third Watch* on a fairly regular basis, responded to the World Trade

Center attack. They didn't make it back. I saw these guys (the last day of shooting before Sept. 11), and then never saw them again."

"The decision to air the special was an easy one," John Wells says. "There was no way to fictionalize it that made any sense, or would not seem inappropriate, but we realized what would be appropriate is to allow them to tell their own stories." Figuring out how to weave the events into the lives of the show's characters was much more difficult, but Wells says the officers and firefighters who work with the show urged the cast and crew to get back to work. "I can only tell you that the people we have always depended upon have been after us to get back on the air, and deal with some of the issues they're concerned about. The firefighters ran into a burning building while thousands managed to get out, these are people who cared deeply about their jobs," Wells said. He added that the nature of the show made it impossible to ignore the real-life terror. Others say the show, largely ignored by critics, may stand to benefit from a new affection for heroes.

Returning to the fictionalized-drama format, the second episode, titled *September 10th* (official season premiere on October 22, 2001) concerned the lives of the World Trade Center "heroes" on the day before the tragedy, up to and including the morning of the attacks. The episode ended with the realization of what had happened, and the firefighters from the old and new shifts climbing aboard the engines and responding. This episode shows the fire crew of 55's at the proper shift change of 9:00am. The third episode, titled *After Time*, saluted the heroes of 9/11, with the firefighters, medics, and cops battling through their own personal emotions and misgivings toward their hero status a week after the tragedies, and spending every free moment at "the pile" searching for their missing friends, including four members of Camelot's Day tour. We also learn that firefighter/paramedic Alex Taylor's father, a Battalion Chief, is missing. Their E-1 engine, which was destroyed in the attack, was replaced by an old Mack, a 1969 CF

600 pumper, presumably from the academy, and replaced by a "new" E-1. Actually it's the same E-1 Hush from season two, which remains on loan to the show.

Five episodes of *Third Watch* were completed prior to the terrorist attacks on 9/11, and two had to be retooled prior to airing. *Blackout*, the original season premiere in which an Arab-American shopkeeper shoots a young African-American shoplifter during a blackout (almost half of the episode was chopped out completely and reshot because according to Wells, some scenes were inappropriate) became the last episode of the season, airing May 13, 2002, instead of September 17th, 2001, as scheduled. The scheduled second episode *Unforgiven*, which ultimately aired April 15, 2002, was also rewritten and reshot to include current events. The original plot centered on firefighter Doherty, and his concerns about being in a hazardous occupation, but was rewritten to be about Officer Sully questioning his faith in God in a series of flashbacks of a shooting incident.

One of the last episodes of the season, *Two hundred and Thirty-Three Days* takes place eight months after the World Trade Center disaster. Firefighter/paramedic Alex Taylor (Amy Carlson) learns that the body of her father, a FDNY Battalion Chief, has been recovered from the site. This prompts a reunion of her mother Veronica Hamel, her uncle, FDNY Ladder Co. Lt. Mike Dolan (Bruce Weitz), and her father's best friend FDNY Lt. Tommy Burns (Ed Marinaro), all from *Hill Street Blues*. In this episode we also see the names of the four members of Camelot Station that were lost in the WTC attack, as they are memorialized on a plaque installed in the firehouse. The four names were Joe Beyer, Tommy Doyle, Sean O'Riordon, and Patrick Pesce, although I'm not sure what these names represent, as they are not actual names of firefighters lost that day.

In a bizarre twist for the ambulance units of *Third Watch*, two Middle Eastern-looking men tried to buy a replica FDNY ambulance from a movie-prop company, according to the *New York Post*. A month later, on May 17, 2002, an anonymous Pakistani emailer contacted a New Jersey ambulance company about buying an ambulance, and running a rescue squad. A law enforcement spokesman says there is no evidence that terrorists sent the e-mail, just as there is no evidence that the two Middle Eastern-looking men who tried to buy a TV ambulance are terrorists.

The e-mail message is the second ambulance-related incident in the area, which the FBI is investigating. They are also looking into the June 11 visit to the New Jersey location of Movie Time Cars, a prop company that rents replicas of fire trucks, ambulances, and police cars to TV and movie producers, in which two men tried to buy an ambulance vehicle similar to the one used on *Third Watch*. According to Sandra Carroll, a spokes-woman for the Newark FBI office, this visit triggered a series of alerts to police and rescue agencies in northern New Jersey and New York, that terrorists might try to use emergency vehicles or look-alikes to carry out attacks.

"Movie Time does not have actual ambulances or police cars, but the replicas are authentic enough that they can pass for the real thing," said Joe Sargo, the company's owner. "For all intents and purposes, what they wanted looked like an ambulance," Sargo added. According to the Associated Press, The Middle Eastern maintenance worker, who offered to pay cash, had said he wanted to buy a replica ambulance in which to store his tools.

ABOUT THE FDNY AND SEPTEMBER 11

"This is going to be the worst day of our lives."
- Dan Nigro, Chief of Operations, to Pete Ganci, Chief of the FDNY

Of the three hundred and forty-three FDNY personnel lost, several were second, and even third generation, firefighters.

"When the alarm is pulled, the firefighters leave the station, not knowing what is waiting for them or what they will be called upon to do."
- Dennis Smith, Author and retired FDNY firefighter

Fathers lost sons, brothers lost brothers, and sons lost fathers.

Among the thousands lost in the terrorist destruction of the World Trade Center Complex were three hundred and forty-one New York City Firefighters and two FDNY Paramedics (leaving 1,138 children fatherless). This number is broken down with approximately one hundred twenty-one in or near the North Tower (first hit), and approximately two hundred twenty-two in or near the South Tower (second hit and first to collapse). Seventeen of the firefighters killed were probationary firefighters with less than nine months on the job; for some it was their first day out of school, and on the job in an actual firehouse. "In all, sixty of the three hundred and forty-one firefighters lost on 9/11 had been off-duty when they responded," states Fire Department spokesman Frank Gribbon. One hundred and eighty-six firefighters were injured, many requiring hospitalization. Over eight hundred firefighters working the site in the days and months following the attack, during the Search and Rescue operations, are unable to return to work due to health problems.

Also killed was a member of the NY Fire-Rescue Patrol. The Fire Patrol is a separate entity. They are paid by the NY Fire Underwriters, and they wear FDNY type turnouts and have voice and radio links to the Dispatcher. They also monitor all runs in the city for possible responses, but they aren't actually FDNY.

In addition, two EMT's from New York-Presbyterian University Hospital, one EMT from Cabrini Hospital, one EMT from Metrocare Ambulance, and one each from Hunter Ambulance, and Forest Hills Volunteers were killed. The total number of EMS personnel injured was one hundred sixteen, including sixty-five from the FDNY, and fifty-one voluntary and private ambulance workers.

There were also twenty-three NY Police Officers (fourteen of which were ESU), thirty-seven New York/New Jersey Port Authority Police Officers, thirty-eight staff workers, three NY State Court Officers, and eleven WTC Security Guards employed by Summit Security Services died that day. A Port Authority police dog trained in explosive detection - a yellow Labrador retriever named Sirius - whose handler kept him inside their office in the basement of the south tower also died in the collapse.

A reality program titled *Murder in Small Town X* featured New York firefighter Angel Juarbe Jr. He was the winner of the Fox Network's reality show, who won $250,000 and a Jeep Liberty on national TV earlier in the year for solving the reality show's semi-scripted murder mystery. Juarbe, 35, a Bronx native, and seven-year veteran of Ladder Co. 12 at 146 W. 19th Street in Manhattan, was one of New York's bravest, and sadly a casualty of 9/11.

According to Tom McDonald, Assistant Commissioner of Fleet and Technical Services, FDNY lost ninety-one pieces of apparatus, and many more were damaged but repairable. Some of the lost equipment includes: Three 1000-gal/min squad pumpers with special tools, four pumpers with 3-stage high-pressure pumps, and twenty

1000-gal/min pumpers. Also one satellite unit with a 2000-gal/min pump and deck gun, six, seventy-five foot tower ladders, twelve, hundred-foot rear-mount ladders, ten ambulances, two heavy rescue units, one tactical support rescue unit providing a 9000-watt light tower, a twenty-five KW generator, Stanley hydraulic system, a fourteen foot motorboat, and a Field Communications Unit. Also lost were two high-rise units that provide crash carts, electric light generators, and one-hour cylinders. Four step vans that provide Haz Mat support, one mask service unit containing three hundred SCBA cylinders, two road-side emergency trucks that provide truck repair capabilities, two EMS Suburbans, used by roving supervisors, and carry extra supplies, twenty-four sedans used by staff chiefs (Ford Crown Victoria or Chevrolet Caprice), and seventeen Suburbans, used by Battalion Chiefs.

FDNY's Field Communications Unit 2, which is staffed by two FDNY civilian dispatchers, was sent to the incident when the signal was sounded for the high-rise fire that erupted after the first airliner attack. One dispatcher was injured, and the FCU vehicle was heavily damaged by falling debris when Tower #1 collapsed. FDNY press office reported that a Jersey City (NJ) fire dispatcher died during the collapse of the South tower. He hitched a ride with three other Jersey City firefighters in their personal vehicle, and was hit by debris while he was getting out of the truck. The other three firefighters were uninjured.

Seagrave Fire Apparatus of Clintonville, Wisconsin rushed to build fifty-four custom fire trucks for New York, after receiving an emergency order in October estimated at 25 million dollars. They will replace some of the ninety-eight pieces of equipment burned, mangled, and crushed when the towers came down. The order consists of seventeen rear-mount aerial trucks, five tillered trucks, four Hi-Pressure pumpers, three Squads, nineteen pumpers, and six Seagrave chassis with Aerialscope tower ladders. The first four apparatus were completed, and driven to New York for acceptance tests on January 22, 2002. Seagrave Fire Apparatus Inc., acquired by FWD Corp. 40 years ago, has been supplying fire equipment to New York since 1918, when some city trucks were still drawn by horses.

Pierce Manufacturing Inc., of Appleton, Wisconsin donated an air and lighting support rescue vehicle to the Fire Department of New York. Built on a Kenworth chassis, the truck bears a special vehicle identification number 9-11-01. In April 2002, the FDNY accepted the donation of a $750,000 custom built apparatus from Airbus. It will go into service as Rescue 1. The specifications were written by Captain Terrance Hatton (Captain Man-Hatton) who was killed on 9/11, along with eleven other members of Rescue 1. Many other departments, manufacturers, and businesses are also involved in replacing some of New York's equipment, as part of the nation's outpouring of support for New York firefighters.

FDNY's Fleet and Technical Services Division returned over one hundred seventy damaged apparatus, cars, light vehicles, and ambulances into service, which were repaired and reequipped during a remarkable one-week period following the WTC disaster. Thirty-nine Ford diesel Excursions, used primarily as Battalion Chief vehicles, have been ordered. An order of eight ninety-five foot Seagrave/Aerialscope towers was already in place along with nineteen 2001 Seagrave hundred-foot rear mounts, some of which have already been delivered. A Salisbury hazardous-materials truck, built on a two-door Mack MR chassis, was delivered in September 2001, for assignment as the first replacement piece for Hazardous Materials Company 1. A 2001 American LaFrance Eagle 1000-gpm pumper was also delivered in September. Originally intended to be on loan for evaluation purposes, FDNY purchased this unit, and it was assigned to Engine Company 34. This is the first American LaFrance pumper to enter FDNY service since 1983.

A year later all the apparatus destroyed in the WTC attack has been replaced. All of the "donated" apparatus has also been placed into service; from apparatus manufacturers, various cities across the country, and monies raised by schoolchildren. One hundred Horton ambulances on Ford F-350 chassis have been ordered.

Within the three hundred twelve square miles of New York City, there are over 825,000 buildings, with new ones going up all the time. Of these, approximately 1265 are commercial and 5,000 are residential buildings, over seventy-five feet in height. They range from 2,000 to 300,000 square feet at ground level. These high-rise structures have added a whole new dimension to the complexities of fire fighting. The Twin Tower building complex had one acre of office space per floor, both towers were one hundred ten stories, and were the third tallest buildings in the world. Once again, the Empire State Building regains its title of tallest building in New York at one hundred three stories. The observation deck is on the eighty-sixth floor.

The FDNY fields 8,500 uniformed firefighters and 3,000 officers, on two hundred ten engines (pumpers), one hundred forty-one ladder trucks, five heavy rescues, seven Squads, three Field Communications vehicles, one Haz Mat, four fireboats, and hundreds of support vehicles, including 3,000 EMS staff on one hundred sixty-nine BLS and fifty-two ALS ambulances. The crew of each engine, truck, rescue, and fireboat constitutes one company. These companies are organized into fifty-four battalions and twelve divisions, which cover the five boroughs of the city in two hundred twenty-five firehouses.

CHAPTER SEVEN — 2000's

For the new millennium an independent production company, TMG/5Artists, began production in September 2000 on *The C-Shift;* a film about a veteran Los Angeles City Fire Department Paramedic, Greg Harbinger, one of the department's brightest members. Unbeknownst to many of his colleagues, including his partner, he continues to suffer the haunting memories of a hot Los Angeles night in April 1992. He feels he failed himself, the department, and his fellow colleagues. However, his time for exorcism will come on a routine run which ironically falls just hours away from the anniversary of the night in question.

Starring Kenny McClain as Harbinger, *The C-Shift* was written by screenwriter Chin Thammasaengsri, who began his career penning scripts predominantly featuring characters in the LAPD & LA City Fire Department. Chin appears as Captain David Hurst in the movie. This film was born out of a number of stories heard, and situations witnessed by Chin while acting as an independent photographer during the Los Angeles Riots of 1992. The drama looks back at that first hellish night of the riots, from the point of view of several Los Angeles City Fire Department Firefighters and Paramedics. One firefighter's internal struggles and tribulations reflect the struggle a city has gone through since that night on April 29, 1992.

Writer and Executive producer, Thammasaengsri states *"The C-Shift* was designed as an independent film, however I have been giving some thought to packaging it up with some of my other written work, and marketing it as a TV pilot. I already have one production company I can pitch it to when it is done." The film was shot at "old" LA City station 46 at 1438 W. Vernon Ave. near the Coliseum, as Station 30. Apparatus used in the film were "retired, worn-out, dead on their feet (wheels), purchased from the LAFD for $1.00," according to the producer. They are a 1970 Seagrave, shop number 60253 which last saw service at LA City Station 33, and a 1980 Ford Econoline van RA (Rescue Ambulance) originally assigned to LAFD West Valley District. The equipment is actually stationed at old 46's and used for fairs and other functions to promote recruitment to the LAFD. "The film is nearing completion, and we suspect will be rolled out in the fall of 2003," states Thammasaengsri, who has penned scripts for Star Trek TNG, DS9, and Voyager. He will be submitting scripts to *Third Watch* (season four), and Star Trek Enterprise. Westlake Signal Group and TMG/5 Artists produced the film, with Raul Moreno as Technical Advisor. Promos for *The C-Shift* began airing on TV in summer 2002.

I wasn't sure where to slot this one in; ***Superfire***, a $15 million dollar ABC production, was produced in Canada, and filmed along the Gold Coast of Queensland, Australia, the state forest reserves on the Sunshine Coast, and in Tokoroa, New Zealand. The show is about American Smoke Jumpers, and air tanker pilots. The miniseries that wasn't, at least in the US, was originally written to air as a three part sixty-minute miniseries (or four part, depending on which release you read).

The drama follows an elite team of forest firefighters battling a superfire, a natural phenomenon with "the energy release of an atomic bomb." Three separate fires, merging into one large "Superfire" surround a small town near Portland, Oregon, and threaten to engulf it. *Superfire* stars D.B. Sweeney (*Once and Again*) as disgraced airplane pilot, James Merrick, who hopes to compensate for a past misdeed, which cost several lives, by volunteering to help fight the fires that threaten to destroy an isolated Oregon community.

Superfire also stars Diane Farr (*Roswell, The Job*) as a tanker pilot, and Wes Studi as the veteran smoke jumper who leads the team. Written by brothers Richard (*Crisis in the Hot Zone*) and Doug

(*The Relic*) Preston, who team up to give us a glimpse into the world of firefighters in extraordinary circumstances.

The show is produced by Stephanie Germain, for Stephanie Germain Productions (Canada) in association with Mandalay Television (US), and Lions Gate Television (Canada – *Dark Angel*). It is directed by Steven Quayle, (*T-2, Titanic, The Abyss*), with music by Russ Landau (*Survivor*). *Superfire* began production in New Zealand in April 2001. The Muriwai Volunteer Fire & Emergency Service of New Zealand was called out to the set one evening, as they were doing a very realistic nighttime shoot in the forest, which alerted the authorities. 111 is New Zealand's equivalent of America's 911.

The miniseries, originally set to air for a winter 2002 release in the US, aired April 20, without much notice, in a shortened ninety-six minute version. It ranked poorly in the ratings, coming eighty-ninth in the Nielsen's, as it was preempted in several markets. A press release issued in Germany lamented the fact that German actor Gedeon Burkhard, as one of the forest service pilots, would not be seen at all in the (unexplained) shortened US version. The miniseries aired in Germany on August 15th and 16th titled *Superfire: Inferno in Oregon*. There is also a two hundred ten minute version for European release. *Superfire* has been sold to several European distributors, and to Japan where it will air as two ninety-minute programs. It's also available on VHS and DVD in the U.S. version.

From the fiction of *Superfire* to fact in Arizona, where thousands were evacuated as Arizona fires beared down on the town of Show Low, after two separate fires merged into one. Beginning on June 18 and 20, 2002, the two fires raged unchecked through the paper-dry Arizona Pine and Juniper forest, and merged into a single blaze of over 300,000 acres, which threatened to burn down the evacuated town. Before they came together on the 23rd of June 2002, the blazes destroyed about one hundred eighty-five homes in eastern

Arizona, and as many as 25,000 people had fled more than half a dozen towns, including Show Low, population 7,700.

The fires centered on an area one hundred twenty-five miles northeast of Phoenix. Initially, nearly 1,600 firefighters and other personnel battled the flames, but were unable to hold a single line of defense as it raced towards Show Low, due to the tinder dry conditions, high winds, and a fifty mile front fire line. By fire's containment on July 8th, it had consumed almost 500,000 acres, destroyed four hundred sixty-seven homes, although luckily the town of Show Low was spared. At its peak, 32,000 people from nine communities were evacuated, and over 4,500 firefighters were on the line. These two devastating fires were started by a lost hiker signaling a rescue helicopter, and by a contract firefighter to earn some extra money fighting fires. A news chopper rescued the hiker, and the volunteer firefighter was arrested for arson.

NBC gave a thirteen-episode commitment to **Romeo Fire**, a thirty-minute sitcom about a group of small-town firefighters. The ensemble comedy follows a group of four firefighters - three men and a woman - who haven't seen a fire in years. "It's basically Friends in the firehouse," says NBC Entertainment President, Jeff Zucker. The show was created, written, and produced by Greg Malins (*Friends*) for a September 2002 debut for Warner Brothers Television and NBC Studios. Preliminarily scheduled for a possible Thursday slot Greg Malins says, "I'm extremely happy at the progress we've made, and the state of the show. There were times when I thought this show wasn't going to work, but we've shot the first few episodes and it definitely works. The cast is all perfect, and it really is very funny. I can't wait to get this show on air and see what the viewers feel. I'm very happy with it, and I think everyone will be too."

The firefighters are Jerry O'Connell (*Sliders, Crossing Jordan*), Steven Dunham, David Ramsey, and Jessica Capshaw, (actress

Kate Capshaw's daughter). Kevin S. Bright, also of *Friends*, directs the show. During production the series title has been stated both as *RomeFire* and *Romeo U.S.A*. The pilot, filmed on April 11th, 2002, was shot in front of a live audience at the Warner Brothers studios in Burbank, California. It is unknown how many episodes other than the pilot were actually filmed.

In the promo, Warner Brothers says, "The show revolves around four firefighters who live and work in the small town of Romeo. Since their actual firefighting duties are few and far between, they end up taking care of the town more than anything else. One of the guys is in love with his female best friend, but she is in love with the new guy, who's obviously still hooked on his ex-wife. There's a guy whose enthusiasm for fires prevents him from passing the psychological exam at every big fire department to which he applies. There's the married mayor, who has a hard time hiding his romantic feelings for one of the firefighters, and there's also a Russian mail order bride. Ultimately, the show is about how when you work in a job like this, your co-workers end up being more your family than even your family."

There are at least five small communities/villages named Romeo in the US, which have populations of 3,000 or less. I wonder which one they are using as a model? In an inquiry, Warner Brothers was looking for a firehouse for their exterior establishing shots. "An old fire station, preferably all brick, but will consider other exteriors. Two story, and should just have one main front door. Ideally, it would be the old fashion kind of door that is split in the middle, and opens outward. Can be in or near small town, with sort of midwestern feel." The production company was hoping to get some feedback from Washington State. I am not sure which station they finally ended up using for the establishing shot.

During the fall schedule releases in May, NBC never mentioned *Romeo Fire* - fall, mid-season or otherwise...so it's looking more and more like the series will end up on the shelf next to all the other unaired pilots. Plus Jessica Capshaw became a regular in ABC's *The Practice* in 2002. Jerry O'Connell is still a semi-regular on NBC's *Crossing Jordan* and discussing a *Crossing Jordan* spin-off with his detective Woody Hoyt character.

BOOMTOWN an ensemble drama set in Los Angeles featuring LAPD cops and detectives, a paramedic, (although not identified as an LA City medic by the generic uniform and badge she is wearing), a reporter, and the Deputy LA District Attorney. The NBC/Dreamworks SGA Television series premiered Sept 29, 2002. The City of Los Angeles threatened to take Boomtown to court unless they paid for the privilege of using the Los Angeles Police Department's name and logos. Occasionally there are firefighters and equipment in the program but they are not regular members of the cast and only serve as background. According to Cinema Vehicle Services who is supplying equipment for the program, Boomtown is not using LAFD logos on the fire and ambulance apparatus but replica or 'look-a-likes', if used at all. The paramedic, Theresa Ortiz, (Lana Parrilla, *Spin City*) is not an integral part of the program. Her partner, listed as a guest star, Randy, no last name (Anthony Diaz-Perez, *Passions*) rarely seen, has little if any speaking lines. There were three different ambulances that were painted and lettered differently in the first three episodes of the season. As of this writing, the ambulance is painted all red and lettered "LA Fire Department" and "LA Fire Dept". There is a Technical Advisor for the PD but none for the fire/paramedic.

Early on in the series it was unknown to what station the paramedic was assigned. Later when fire apparatus are seen, it is Engine 54 and Truck 54 arriving with the medic wearing fire gear with '54' on her helmet. It is typical with movies and TV programs to not utilize actual in-service fire station numbers. The real LA City Station 54 has been out of service since 1989. This same equipment has been seen on Fox's ***24***, ***Diagnosis Murder's*** "Malibu Fire", and

"Point of Origin" (2002). It's provided by Joe Ortiz of Fire Equipment Rental.

Lana Parrilla in *Boomtown*
NBC Photo

CHAPTER EIGHT—
NON-FIREFIGHTER THEMED SERIES WITH FIREFIGHTER CHARACTERS; STARRING OR RECURRING

Leave it to Beaver had a fireman in a semi-recurring role. The original *Leave it to Beaver*, which aired from 1957-1958 on CBS, and 1958-1963 on ABC featured "Gus the Fireman." Gus from Fire Station 7 with his Dalmatian, "Chief," would often be giving the Beaver advice on overcoming his fears and problems of the day. Gus, played by Burt Mustin appeared in fourteen episodes, and would later be seen in *Emergency!* episode 4:22, and *905-Wild*.

Petticoat Junction, a CBS series that aired from 1963 to 1970, in which Uncle Joe (Edgar Buchanan) who lived in the hotel, was also the Volunteer Fire Chief of Hooterville. The other two members of the department, Smiley Burnette as Captain Charlie Pratt, and Rufe Davis as Secretary Floyd Smoot, were also the engineer and conductor on the Cannon Ball Express. Motel chain Holiday Inn issued a "Member in good standing certificate" to the Hooterville Volunteer Fire Department.

Tony and Golden Globe recipient Brian Dennehy (*Rambo: First Blood, Cocoon*) has starred in two very short-lived fire-related series. ***Star of the Family***, a half-hour sitcom debuted on ABC September 30, 1982, and only ran two episodes. Dennehy played a firefighter, although the show was not about firefighting. *Star of the Family* was mostly about his teenage daughter, Kathy Maisnik, a sixteen-year-old (played by a twenty year old) country singer whose budding career complicated her family life. They lived at 7136 La Salle Drive in an unnamed city in Southern California. Dennehy, whose wife has run off with a hotel manager, played the protective but proud father, a fire captain with his "strange" crew at the firehouse, which one critic said was like "Barney Miller set in a firehouse." Danny Mora, Todd Susman, and George Deloy played other firefighters at Engine Co. 64. The series was co-created by Rick Mitz, author of *The Great TV Sitcom Book*. Ironically, the show was nominated for "Best New Family Television Series" and Kathy Maisnik as "Best Young Actress in a New TV Series" at the 4th Annual Young Artist Awards in 1983.

In the second series, which debuted on NBC in March 2001, Dennehy, plays a widower and retired FDNY Fire Captain in the half-hour comedy *The Fighting Fitzgeralds*. As head of this Irish Catholic family living in Long Island, New York, he owns and operates a bar, and has to deal with his three grown sons, one of whom is going through the firefighter-testing process. This 10-episode series filmed in front of a live audience in Burbank, California, aired on Tuesdays at 8:00pm, initially drawing good reviews, but eventually suffered poor ratings, making way for the US version of *The Weakest Link*. Created by Brian Burns, *The Fighting Fitzgeralds* was produced by Irish Twins and Mauretania Productions, in association with Artist Television Group.

I mention these non-firefighter themed programs as Dennehy, short of becoming typecast, again plays a firefighter in three (so-far) episodes of *Just Shoot Me*. Dennehy has a semi-recurring role as Red Finch, *Blush* office manager, Dennis Finch (David Spade's) macho fireman father, who attempts to reestablish a relationship with the son he thinks is gay, because he's not a big butch firefighter like his other two sons. He will be back in the 2002/2003 season as well.

The Boys is a thirty-minute comedy about a young writer, Christopher Meloni (*Law & Order, SVU, Oz*) and his girlfriend, who move into a dead man's house in Seattle, Washington, and inherit three surviving friends. He plays poker with the three old men who live next door. One of the old men is a retired firefighter, played by Ned Beatty, while Doris Roberts (*Everybody Loves Raymond*) plays Beatty's wife. The series filmed six episodes excluding the pilot, although the pilot and sixth episode never aired. The series ran from August 20, through September 1993 on CBS, and was created, written, and produced by Dan O'Shannon.

The Family Man (from the creators of *Full House*) was filmed before a live audience, and starred Gregory Harrison (*Trapper John, MD*). The comedy took place in the fictional Southern California community of Eagle Ridge, where Harrison, a widower raising his four kids on 6521 Oak Valley Lane, is a Fire Captain at Eagle Ridge Fire Station 27. It ran on CBS from Sept. 11, 1990 through July 1991. Produced by Lorimar Productions, with music by Steven Chesne.

Family Man promos
CBS Photo

Kelly Kelly, a comedy starring Shelley Long (*Cheers*) and Robert Hays (*Airplane* movies) as her husband, a fire Captain with the Norbrook, New Jersey Fire Department. They meet when he rescues her from a building, and by the third episode they are getting married. There is some firehouse activity, and one episode with his daughter wanting to become a firefighter. The 7-episode series debuted April 20, 1998 at 7:00pm on the WB Network. In association with Utility Pictures, Itzbeenso Long Productions produced the show for Warner Brothers. Shelley Long and David Kendall created the program. The apparatus in the firehouse was an old Seagrave. The working title was, *"Put the Seat Down"*.

PROVIDENCE starring Melina Kanakaredes, as Dr. Syd Hansen, aired on NBC January 1999 – Dec 2002. Some establishing exterior shots are filmed in Providence, RI but primarily filmed in the

Paula Cale as Joanie Hansen, Jon Hamm as Fireman Burt in *Providence*. NBC photo by Paul Drinkwater

Los Angeles, CA area. In season two and three, Burt Ridley (Jon Hamm) had a reoccurring role as a Providence firefighter appearing in 16 episodes. He saves Joanie Hansen's life (Syd's younger sister) during a fire in her store and begin dating shortly there after.

While firefighters have appeared on the Emmy award winning program, *Sesame Street* in the past, it was the beginning of its 33rd season that bears mention here. On February 4, 2002, the first four episodes dealing with the World Trade Center disaster were created in response to the tragedy. In the first episode, FDNY firefighters arrive at Mr. Hooper's store in response to a fire in the kitchen. Elmo returns to the firehouse of Engine 58/Ladder 26, nicknamed the "Fire Factory" in Harlem, where he tours the firehouse and learns about fire safety. Other episodes deal with fear, stress, and loss. In the end, the children get an inside look at the "real-life" home of firefighters.

CHAPTER NINE — ON THE DRAWING BOARD

Since *Emergency!* Randolph Mantooth has guest starred as a firefighter in two other shows; in Richard Dean Anderson's *MacGyver* in the episode titled *The Prometheus Syndrome*, which aired October 7th, 1991, as an LA City Fire Department fire inspector. Randy's character is killed early on in the episode, as a result of a bomb explosion set off by a psychopathic arsonist for revenge against firefighters. MacGyver uses a firefighter's badge to get out of one of his infamous jams. LA City station 27 was used for the exteriors. Later, Randy guest starred as a volunteer firefighter in an episode of *Diagnosis Murder* on October 2nd, 1997, titled "Malibu Fire", as has been previously mentioned.

Randy is currently in the development and production stages for a TV pilot titled **USAR-1**. It's based on a real **U**rban **S**earch **A**nd **R**escue team of the LA County Fire Department. Kevin Tighe will have a recurring role in the series if it is picked up, which will be the first time they have worked together since *Emergency!* The two will NOT be reprising their *Emergency!* characters. "Anyone expecting *USAR—1* to pick up where *Emergency!* left off will be disappointed," says Randy.

After receiving approval from LA County Fire Chief, P. Michael Freeman, Randy and the show's producer did several ride-alongs with LA County's USAR 103 to learn more about USAR and the roll they play in the fire service. *USAR-1* promises to be similar to the *Emergency!* series in only one aspect, its realistic and dramatic portrayal of LA County Fire Department operations. The show will draw its storylines and technical advisors from real USAR stories and personnel. They even intend to use actual footage of LACoFD responses.

In an October 1999 interview, Mantooth said, "In our show, *USAR-1*, the team consists of a Captain, an Engineer, and two firefighter specialists on a twenty-eight ton USAR rig. The other part of the team, which is called "Air Ops," consists of a pilot (who is not a fireman), and two firefighter/paramedic crewmen. They are trying to outfit USAR-1 with Sikorsky (UH-60) Black Hawk helicopters. Believe me, it is a truly awesome sight to see this team attack a rescue, both from the ground and the air. We are going to try to be as responsible with *USAR-1* as Bob Cinader was with *Emergency!* There are two women in our show, and one dog."

He went on to say, "At this time we are not writing scripts, we're just developing the show, its concept, and its characters. This is all the networks are interested in. If they like the idea, they ask for the scripts. I may have some influence, but I do not have the final say. I plan on being an actor in it, the Captain of the USAR squad. I will also be the executive producer, along with three or four others. Then maybe I can get behind the camera, and direct a couple. But my true desire lies in seeing *USAR-1* on screen, the sooner the better."

"There are some things about a show that have to be kept secret," stated Randy, "And Kevin's participation as an actor in the show has to be kept under wraps for the time being, but don't miss the first episode (intriguing, isn't it?). Kevin's one of my best friends, and we haven't worked together in twenty years - that alone is enough to look forward to," he said.

It was pitched to CBS in late 1999 for a possible Fall 2000 release, which unfortunately did not take place. In 2001, it was pitched to other networks, and as of this writing they have talked with the USA Network.

In August of 2001, Cosgrove-Meurer Productions in Burbank, California, was looking for female firefighters/paramedics for a new Lifetime Television series program entitled *Search and Rescue*. The program is designed to profile the lives and work of women who have dedicated themselves to helping others. Their casting call stated that they were "Looking for women who have stories to tell of a successful rescue or lifesaving event, which epitomizes the work they do; an event that has made all the hard work, harassment, and stress worthwhile.

Such an event might be saving someone from a burning building, reviving a young drowning victim, keeping someone alive after being trapped in a car following a devastating car accident, or pulling someone off a rooftop during a flood. Incidents that were covered by the news media are preferable, although it is not necessary that the actual rescue was caught on tape." Filming was scheduled for August 2001, and it is unknown if the series was developed.

CHAPTER TEN — REALITY TV PROGRAMS

US shows like *Rescue 911* and *Code 3*, as well as foreign programs such as Britain's *999* are commonly called "Reality TV" programs, which are a mix of re-enactments and/or actual footage of the incident. Prior to a pilot, filmed in 1954, titled *Alarm* (see chapter one), there was an episodic series titled **Man Behind the Badge**. The 91-episode crime/drama series was a dramatization of actual case stories from around the US, mainly police-related but with several fire-related incidents.

One story featured Houston Texas Fire Investigator, Chief Harry A. Foster on the trail of "The Elusive Firebug." The thirty-minute CBS series produced by Revere Studios, aired from November 1953 through September 1955. Hosted by actor Charles Bickford, and directed by Paul Landres (*Maverick, Adam-12*) it was syndicated around the world. The series also featured Anthony Perkins, Millburn Stone, and Leslie Nielsen in early roles. A spin-off sixty-minute TV movie with the same title was made in 1955.

Other strictly fire-related programs were: the thirty-minute syndicated program **On Scene: Emergency Response** (1990-1994), with one hundred four episodes produced by Dave Forman. In 1996, **Fire Rescue: Emergency Response**, a 22-episode series, was basically the same program format but with a title change. The latter was produced by 4M Productions, and Dave Forman, who did his stand-ups in fire gear in front of the featured fire department, hosted both shows.

Other shows, although not totally fire or EMS-related, but include fire and rescue scenes were: **Survival** (1964), hosted by James Whitmore Jr.; **Emergency Call** (1991-1992), hosted by Joseph Campanella; **I Witness Video** (1992-1994), hosted by Patrick Van

Horn and John Forsythe, and *Real TV* (1996 and still airing), television's first all-video caught-on-camera series now in its sixth season. First hosted by Emmy award-winning journalist, John Daly, and now by Emmy award-winner, Ahmad Rashad, *Real TV* is seen in two hundred ten markets in the United States, and internationally in twenty-five countries.

When Disaster Strikes first aired in October 1996 on Fox, and was hosted by Martin Sheen, who presented an hour of jet crash, flooding, hurricane, firefighting, avalanche, and tornado footage, and the survivor's stories. A year later Peter Coyote would host. Also from Fox Television came *Emergency Rescue,* a pilot/spec, as the show was being pitched in case of the writers strike for release February 2001. This sixty-minute reality program produced by Richard Wortman (*Real TV*) for Pursuit Productions Inc. never aired.

Emmy award-winning journalist Alex Paen hosted *Emergency with Alex Paen,* a half-hour series that went behind-the-scenes, focusing on the heroic actions of firefighters, police, and rescue workers, who protect and save people from disasters and accidents. First airing in 1994, thirty-three thirty-minute episodes, produced by Telco Productions, Inc. and CBS Broadcast International, have aired worldwide, and are still in syndication today. Formerly with ABC TV in Los Angeles, Paen has covered national and international news events around the globe, from the Middle East to Africa, Asia, and Latin America. He currently hosts *Animal Rescue*, where instead of covering people, his cameras travel around the world featuring dramatic animal rescue stories.

In *Firefighters*, "the firefighters are the stars, not the fire… these are stories about people saving lives," according to Executive Producer Al Korn, former CEO of RKO Pictures.

Production began in late 1992 for this reality-based program, which premiered January 23rd, 1993. It was shot primarily in New York City along with Philadelphia and Detroit. Much of the New York ride-along footage was filmed on FDNY's Squad 1, a "freelance" engine that responds to all working alarms within its district (see *Third Watch* Squad 55), and a Rescue Company. One episode featuring the Dade County Florida Fire Department was dedicated to the Hurricane Andrew disaster of August 1992, in which more than sixty people were killed and approximately two million people evacuated their homes.

A videographer would shoot aboard the engine while responding to alarms. When "on scene" he would suit up and go inside with the companies, while a second unit would film the exteriors. Camera crews traveled with the Bureau of Alcohol, Tobacco, and Firearms (ATF), and gained exclusive footage of the February 1993 World

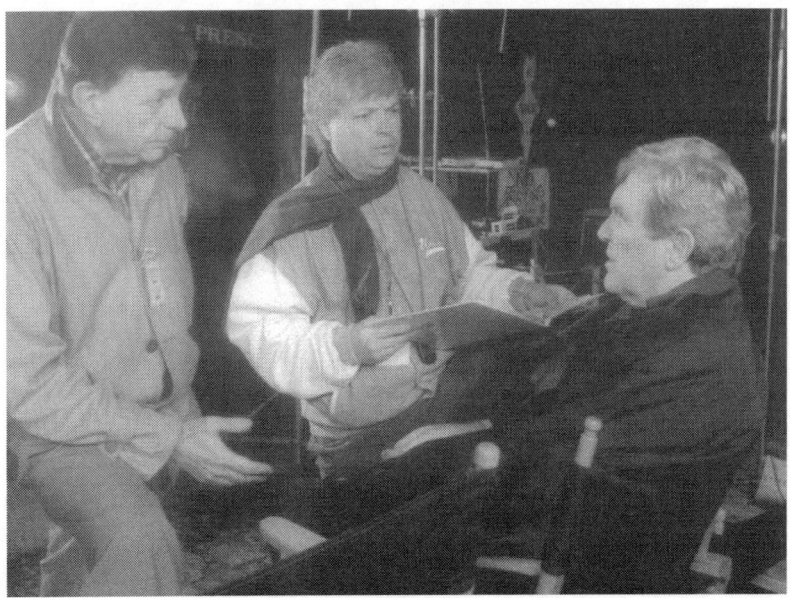

L-R: Al Korn, Tom Lupo and Robert Lansing (seated) going over script for *Firefighters*
Photo courtesy of Tom Lupo

Trade Center bombing where six lives were lost. The show featured a weekly segment on ATF's most-wanted arsonist. One of the program's regular features was *Hero of the Week*, where viewers around the country submitted bystander videos. Host Robert Lansing (*The Equalizer, 12 o'clock High*) would do his stand-ups in New York, and later on the back lot at Universal Studios Florida. It was a thirty-minute program of thirteen original episodes, which ran for 26 weeks, of which some episodes were remixes or repeats. Grove Television Enterprises of Chicago syndicated the show to one hundred twenty-four US markets, including Europe. Created and co-produced by Al Korn and Tom Lupo, and directed by Tom Lupo for Americom International Entertainment Ltd. Head writers were Wendy (Raab) Leonard and Tom Selligson. Technical Advisor was Frank Quinn from the FDNY. Several of the FDNY firefighters featured during this series lost their lives during the attack on the World Trade Center on 9/11.

Steve Greene, Executive Producer with Dalmatian Productions Inc. in Coral Springs Florida, announced the airing of a new reality-based hour-long, international television program, **Rescue Heroes!** "As an integral part of this new program, we will be able to feature video segments from career and volunteer EMS, fire, and rescue departments, not only from the United States, but from around the world. Our international viewing audiences will see the best of the best, the bravest of the brave, from Oregon to the Outback, from the Jersey shore to Japan."

The sixty-minute program is currently in negotiations with several US Cable Networks. It has already aired in parts of Europe, Central and South America, the Middle and Far East, in association with Britain's ZoneVision and UPC's RealityTV channel. "Each episode airs twelve to fourteen segments of real fire/rescues, no re-creations or dramatizations," states Greene. (If you have a significant fire/rescue/EMS incident on video, contact Dalmatian Productions, Inc. Their website is listed in a later chapter).

The Fox Network aired an hour of Emergency Rescues with their special *Code Red: Moment of Survival*. According to the show's Executive Producer, Paul Stojanovich (*Cops, World's Wildest Police Videos, World's Scariest Police Chases, World's Scariest Police Stings, Riots: Out of Control, Surviving the Moment of Impact*), "*Code Red* does for emergency rescues what *Police Videos* does for law enforcement." *Code Red* presented exciting, humorous, and unbelievable videos of real emergency workers involved in real life rescues from around the world. The two hour-long specials, rated TV-14, premiered Friday Feb. 2 and 9, 2002 at 9:00pm.

Further disclaiming PA: Due to the graphic nature of this program, viewer discretion is advised. Narrated by Hank Brandt and hosted by Michael Newman, (*Baywatch* – 1989 to 2000, *L.A. Lifeguards* – 1998). Newman, a LA County Lifeguard since 1977, and an LA County Firefighter since 1985, wears an LA City firefighter uniform in the program, and states that he is not a lifeguard, but "a former firefighter for almost 20 years." Newman is still an active lifeguard and firefighter for LA County. *Code Red* is not on Fox's line-up at this time, as the series was never developed. (It seems Fox and ABC (*Code Red*, 1981), don't understand that *Code Red* is Hospital Code for fire/smoke, or reporting a nuclear accident, and not a fire department term).

A number of individuals function both as lifeguards and firefighters for LA County. Although separate functions, on a given day one would be either a lifeguard or a firefighter. Firefighters function as lifeguards only when staffing requirements warrant overtime. Lateral transfers do not exist at this time. Single role lifeguards who want to become firefighters (or vice versa) must go through the same testing and selection process as everyone else. In 1994, the County Lifeguard Division merged into the County of Los Angeles Fire Department under Fire Chief, P. Michael Freeman.

Dayton, Ohio firefighters star in a Reality-TV series pilot titled *Firefighters*. "The show features four segments that begin with firefighters hanging out in the station, to getting the fire call, to actually being out there at the fire," said J.T. Stewart, the show's writer and director. "When you see the flames, it really gets your heart pumping." The show's pilot was filmed over the past year (2000) in the Dayton area, with fire departments from Dayton, Clark County, Urbana, and Enon, Ohio. The videographer spent about a week- and-a-half at each station.

The post-production for *Firefighters* was completed July 1, 2001 at Showorks Studios in Orlando, Florida. Stewart said Blazing Chase (Blazing Chase Productions, a Dayton-based television production company) has already begun marketing the show to cable networks such as The Learning Channel, Discovery Channel, and Fox. Assuming the show gets picked up, Stewart said filming would expand to other cities across the country, and have about thirteen episodes in the first season.

The Bravest, premiered September 24, 2001, features real stories from real firefighters, a riveting, emotional portrayal of the men and women who work in the world's most dangerous profession ...firefighting. This live-action sixty-minute reality television series documents all aspects of the firefighter's job. Visiting fire departments across North America, *The Bravest* takes viewers to the scenes of disaster— raging fires, car crashes, train accidents, building collapses, and much more. The original concept was forty-four thirty-minute programs featuring one city or Engine Company per show, but producers ultimately combined the segments to produce a full hour featuring two different departments. The series ran fifty-two weeks with select shows being repeated.

The Bravest goes inside the firehouse to see where firefighters live, eat, sleep, and work together. Production crews accompany the firefighters twenty-four hours a day, documenting their words, actions, and every risk, to bring the unseen world of firefighting to the viewer. Equipped with up to seven cameras, the production crews mounted cameras inside of the front cab, on the back step, and on the roofs of fire trucks. On scene, a two-and-a-half pound "Vest Cam" was mounted on the firefighters' air packs to bring viewers to the frontlines of fighting a fire, as well as other handheld cameras. Honoring the heart and soul of the firefighter, cameras capture the true working shift of these men and women, who run into dangerous situations when everyone else runs out!

The premiere episode begins with a dedication to the firefighters who risked their lives, and those who tragically lost their lives in their heroic attempts to rescue victims of the World Trade Center disaster on 9/11. The first episode features Brooklyn's elite Rescue 2, which was shot in May 2001, and San Francisco's Station 7 and Rescue Squad 2 featuring Caroline Paul. The next episode features Rescue 1 - Manhattan and Rescue 2 - Brooklyn. Some of these firefighters were among the first units that responded to the attacks on the World Trade Center. Manhattan's Rescue 1 and Brooklyn's Rescue 2 lost a combined eighteen men that morning; firefighter Daniel Libretti of Rescue 2 was one of them. Ironically, Libretti said on *The Bravest*, "Just when you feel confident in yourself, this job has a way of humbling you. Just when you think you know what you're doing, you get a curve ball thrown at you."

Russell Best, the series' creator, calls the firefighters "The bravest people you could ever imagine meeting. These guys are like — they want the high rise, you know, fires. That's the adrenaline rush. They want to get in there and save people, so we knew that they were down there," Best said. "I really believe that if they sent them to hell, they would put it out, the World Trade Center collapse was worse than hell."

At sixty-three, Joseph Angelini was the oldest active member of the fire department. He had been cited for bravery fourteen times.

People who spent time with him called him a man of few words. He was loved by his colleagues, and fueled by an unwavering desire to save people. "My son, Joe, is over at Ladder 4, which is in the theater district, and we catch fires sometimes together, which is a good thing and it's fun," he told *The Bravest*. Now, Joseph Sr. is dead, and Joseph Jr.'s body was never recovered.

Cities featured in future episodes are Boston, Dallas, Washington DC, Miami, Los Angeles, San Francisco, and more. San Francisco firefighter and author Caroline Paul, twin sister of actress Alexandra Paul (*Fire Co. 132, Baywatch*), is featured in one episode. Hearst Entertainment, Inc. produces *The Bravest*, in association with National Entertainment. Richard Best is Creator and Executive Producer; Tammy Leech is co-Executive Producer for National Entertainment, while Lieutenant Peter M. Sapienza of FDNY Engine 28 is Technical Advisor. The program is syndicated in the US and Ontario, Canada, and aired at various times on Saturdays or Sundays on network and independent stations across the country. Selected episodes are available on VHS and DVD at United American Video at 1-800-486-6782 or by visiting their website at http://www.entermagic.com. Hearst Entertainment told me it was a very expensive series to produce and there wasn't enough interest from the advertising community to support a second season.

Firehouse, a five part series, began airing July 2002, and is produced by Dateline NBC, and narrated by the firefighters in their own words. The program is hosted by former volunteer firefighter and NBC news anchor, Brian Williams. Shot over the course of seven months with small handheld cameras, *Firehouse* follows the lives of men and women in New York, Camden, NJ, Miami Florida, and San Francisco. With cameras attached to firefighter's turnouts, they get into situations where the search for victims is difficult, and you can't see your hands in front of your eyes, as the smoke is so thick.

Firehouse focuses on Rescue companies, and new recruits, and follows one New York firefighter with footage shot eight years ago by Dateline from a rookie firefighter, to the events of September 11. *Firehouse* was to air over the course of five weeks from July 19 through August 16, 2002, but was cancelled after only three episodes due to poor ratings. *Firehouse* ranked forty-seventh and sixty-ninth respectively in its last two airings.

Primarily due to the WTC tie-in, and the anniversary of the attack, the episode featuring FDNY's Engine 25 and Ladder 5 aired September 1, 2002. This particular station lost eleven members on that fateful day in 2001. NBC said the remaining episode on San Francisco might air at some undetermined date in the future. David Corvo is the executive producer of Dateline NBC.

A new series called, *What Should You Do?* features the true stories of women who have survived life-threatening situations and is scheduled to air on the Lifetime Channel beginning March 24, 2003 with 22 episodes. This reality series uses dramatizations to recreate real-life challenges and how to best handle them. For instance: what should you do when someone is choking, or someone has broken into your home, or you're trapped in the trunk of a car, trapped in a fire, etc. According to the producers, on hand to offer the best instruction of how to handle these situations is Charles Ingram, a U.S. Marine/survivalist, Dr. Winnie King, an emergency room doctor and former medical reporter at KCBS-TV, and 22-year FBI veteran, Candice DeLong. They seem to have left out the usual cast of characters such as police, firefighters, and EMT's, who are, by far, the best experts on these everyday things. This program concept is quite similar to England's *999* program airing on BBC-1 since 1992 and discussed in a later chapter. Produced by 44 Blue Productions, in Studio City, CA, has been a supplier of reality, documentary, "how to" and action-adventure programming since 1984.

CHAPTER ELEVEN — DOCUMENTARIES

There have been many programs about disasters dealing with earthquakes, floods, and fires. Several award-winning documentaries specifically showcase a human-interest side of actual firefighters. Touching on only a few, I hope to give some incite into "real" TV firefighters. Many of these fire-related documentary programs, and many more, are available from A&E, the Discovery Channel, TLC, FSP Books and Videos, and many other sources.

New York City's "The-Bronx-is-Burning" arson epidemic of the early '70s was sparked by the fact that owners of otherwise marginal buildings couldn't earn enough from rentals to cover their operating expenses. They were walking away from their buildings in droves; some even torched or set fire to their buildings for insurance proceeds. New York City was teetering on the edge of bankruptcy. One fire station might have ten calls a night, with firefighters going from fire to fire. One New York City firefighter, Dennis Smith, published his first book in 1972, *Report From Engine Co. 82*, about such events, and where he was stationed from 1967 through 1973.

A bestseller for weeks, Smith later founded *Firehouse* magazine. On September 27, 1972, on Britain's BBC-2 Television, a documentary titled ***The Bronx is Burning***, featuring Dennis Smith, was televised in their "Man Alive" series. "A story of a remarkable group of men who belonged to Engine No. 82, Ladder No. 31, and Battalion 27 of the New York Fire Department," the station that Smith had written about in his book. The fifty-two minute program dealt with the daily routines of Engine Co. 82 in the South Bronx, which at the time was the busiest fire station in New York. Frequently their trucks were stoned, and they often had to fight the very people they came to save. "This is the story of the men who fight the fires, and their explanation of what makes their profession so special." The BBC program was produced for BBC-2 by Harry Weisbloom, and narrated by British TV Reporter Jeremy James. Time-Life Films acquired the program in 1974, and Burgess Meredith re-dubbed the narration voice over. The Time-Life version is currently available in 16mm format from the Southwest Michigan Library Cooperative. Dennis Smith retired from the FDNY in 1981, and is an Honorary Assistant Chief of the department.

On the A&E channel, *Firefighters – Real Life Heroes* was presented in two, hour-long programs in 1991 and 1993. The first, *FDNY: Brothers in Battle* takes an unforgettable journey into the lives of the firefighters of New York City, and details the recovery of a plane from the freezing Atlantic Ocean. The program was written and produced by FDNY's Captain Brian Hickey for Startwater Productions, Inc., narrated by Ed Sere, and directed and executive-produced by Raymond P. Hickey, Brian's brother.

The second, *In the Heat of the Blaze*, was presented in 1993, and contains footage of the daily struggles of the firefighters in the Chicago Fire Department. Witness a desperate attempt to free colleagues trapped beneath a collapsed roof, and the rescue of a robbery victim stuffed in an air duct. It also looks at the 1986 Chernobyl tragedy, where a small band of Russian firefighters managed to contain a nuclear meltdown, despite fatal levels of radiation that killed all but one of the responding firefighters.

In 1995, *FDNY: Brothers in Battle* was rewritten slightly by Captain Hickey, renamed *Firefighters – Brothers in Battle*, and narrated by Bill Curtis for A&E. This video takes the viewer from the fire department's training academy on Randalls Island, to the elite rescue units. Rescue 4 in Queens is featured prominently. On September 11, 2001, Captain Hickey of Rescue 4 was working

Rescue 3 on an overtime shift, and was killed at the World Trade Center, as were many other firefighters featured in this video.

ARSON: THE FIRE INVESTIGATORS A documentary on the Fire Investigators of the London Fire Brigade, who are called in to determine whether or not a fire has been started deliberately. Film crews followed London's fire investigators both night and day for a month. The 50-minute documentary first aired March 1995 on Britain's Channel 4. Reviews say of this, "Top Documentary, forget *London's Burning* - the heroic fire investigators do it for real" *The Sun*, "Compelling" *Today*, "Flame-soaring spectacle" *Daily Mail* "A surefire winner, absorbing" *The Times*.

In their "20th Century" series in 1996, A&E's *Fire Storm!* showed the destruction after the major fires in California. First was the fire in Berkley and Oakland Hills in October 1991, which killed twenty-five people, and destroyed 3,000 homes. It was fought by 2,000 firefighters, and caused 7 billion dollars worth of damage. We see 2,000-degree radiant heat causing buildings to literally explode into flames; then the fires in Laguna and Malibu in the autumn of 1993, where firestorm conditions also occurred. Mike Wallace narrated the program.

In 1996, The Learning Channel (TLC) aired a one-part segment titled *Firefighters*. This one-hour program showcased the Boston Fire Department's Engine 52, Ladder 29, and the Recruit Academy.

"Two fires! Two shootings! One rescue!" And that's just in the opening minutes of the hour-long episode of *Streets of Fire*, which aired in England, and had British television viewers enthralled. The three-part series, each an hour long, was filmed in Baltimore, Maryland, and showcased the units of Rescue 1, the Fire Prevention Bureau, and fires in general around the city. The film crew rode along on the engines and trucks to actual events in the city. British filmmaker, Paul Berriff, filmed the series in 1997 for BBC1, and Ben Gale produced the series for Lion Television. On January 4-5, 1998, the Discovery Channel first aired the documentary in the US under the title *Firehouse.*

In October 1998, The USA Network aired an hour-long special titled ***First Response.*** The producers lived with, and followed the crews of LAFD Station 27 in Hollywood, and Station 66 in South LA for three weeks. The network expressed an interest in featuring other cities across the nation, and twenty-eight episodes were ordered. Only about five were completed – in other parts of LA, Chicago, and New York – but were never shown. Henry Winkler ("Fonzie" of *Happy Days*, producer of *MacGyver*) produced the program.

Great North Productions Inc., and GRB Entertainment of Canada, conducted countrywide research for a fifteen-part documentary titled ***Inferno!*** The program first aired in 1998 on Canada's Life Network, featuring a Hi-Rise fire, and again in January 1999 on The Discovery Channel. The program featured all aspects of firefighting, including specialized fire teams, arson, forest fires, oil fires, fires at historical sites, and at public places. A different city was featured in each episode. The documentary was produced by award-winner David McIlvride.

TLC debuted ***Inside the Inferno*** in May 1999. A hard-hitting action documentary, which took the viewer into the stations, lives, and families of firefighters, it featured firefighters from around the world. From Brazilian firefighters searching for wildfires, to those battling the firestorms of Los Angeles, to the amazing rescue of more than seventy people from a burning hotel.

In February 1999, The Discovery Channel aired a two-hour program titled ***Firestorm***. It was a chronicle of firefighters' efforts to control and extinguish the 1998 Florida fires, as well as wildfires in

California and New Mexico. It specifically showcased smoke jumpers (known as the green berets of the Forest Service), hotshot fire crews (the Marines), and Air Tanker personnel (the air force).

Into the Flames, a British-produced documentary for TLC, featured the work of firefighters around the world, and consisted of three hour-long episodes concerned with fire safety. *Fire in the Sky*, *Fire in the City*, and *Forest Fire* ran May through September 1998. Others produced were *Fire in the Hills* in 1999, and *Fire at Sea* in 2000. Louise Roth, producer for Wall To Wall Television Ltd., UK produced the series, while Prof. Galea was the technical consultant.

California's Gold, the only statewide television series in California about California, is a visual travel log featuring interesting places to visit in the Golden State. The 30-minute series, now in its 12th season, is produced and hosted by Huell Howser. Along with KCRT Television in Los Angeles, the series airs on all 13 PBS affiliates in the state and is used in over a thousand schools and libraries as a resource for people to learn more about the state's rich history, cultural diversity and natural wonders. In addition, a one-hour California's Gold Special aired on PBS nationally, and more specials are planned.

Along with airing the well-known and obsure places to visit in the state this program is mentioned as it featured a segment on fire apparatus that has been used in movies and TV programs. The segment titled, "Fire Trucks" which first aired in 2000, states, "If you've ever wondered where old fire trucks go when they retire, here's the show for you. Joe Ortiz (a retired fireman) has collected one of the largest collections of antique and modern fire fighting equipment around. Huell goes on to Joe's house in Shadow Hills for a personal tour and a very special ride in the back of a hook and ladder." Many of the fire trucks have appeared in movies and TV programs, such as 'Diagnosis Murder's *Malibu Fire*, many others, and currently in this season's 'Boomtown'. One of Joe's ambulances is on display at the Los Angeles City Fire Museum at old Station 27. Other fire related programs on California's Gold are on LA Fire Station 35, old Fire Station 30, which is now the location for the African-American Firefighters Museum, and LA's oldest Fire Boat, the 75 year-old Ralph J. Scott. Hewell attended the 2002 National SPAAMFAA (Society for the Preservation and Appreciation of Antique Motor Fire Apparatus in America) Convention where there were all kinds of apparatus from small hand pumpers to elaborate steam driven engines. He ventured into the Sequoia National Forest to visit Buck Rock Fire Lookout, which was one of the first fire detection locations in the Sierra Nevada Mountains, which was built in 1923. These videos are available at California's Gold web site at http://www.calgold.com.

Test of Courage: The Making of a Firefighter was a behind-the-scenes look at the trials and triumphs of a group of young men and women competing to become firefighters. Filmed over the course of three years in Oakland, California – one of the most culturally diverse cities in America – the program follows a cast of aspiring firefighters, men and women, from different ethnic backgrounds, who are competing against 5000 applicants for only 50 jobs. The program gets inside the lives and hearts of these applicants, and shows the grueling training and preparation they go through as the applicant pool gets continually narrowed down. Also, there are elimination tests of physical agility, intellectual preparedness, and a subjective oral interview that goes a long way to determining if the candidate has "the right stuff" for the job.

Test of Courage debuted Sept 3, 2000 on PBS stations across the country. Filmed by the Independent Television Service (ITVS), and produced and directed by Emmy award-winner, Gary Mercer, and award-winning Kyung Sun Yu, in collaboration with The Working Group.

TV Firefighters

Trial By Fire is a new program in the National Geographic "Out There" TV series, which profiles remarkable individuals in the field—explorers who face dangers head on. National Geographic staff photographer, Mark Thiessen, tags along with wildland firefighters in the field facing oppressive conditions, and sometimes even death. Learn what keeps them coming back each summer. *Trial by Fire* began airing in September 2001, and is one of twenty-six new programs in the series shown in forty-two countries worldwide.

WGBH and NOVA present ***Firewomen***, a series of five short segments, with a new episode each week. The documentary chronicles the steps of six women trainees, as they pursue their dreams of saving lives and protecting the public. At the Fire Department Academy on Boston's Moon Island, squads of trainees endure rigorous simulations in all kinds of weather to help prepare them to battle real-world blazes, and face other dangerous situations, where they must prove they can handle the same physically demanding tasks as their male counterparts. Filmed in early 2001, the series premiered in October. Of the sixteen hundred-member force of the Boston FD, only eighteen are female.

Firemen in the Bronx was filmed in 2000 over a fourteen-day period, but did not air until March 2002. The program takes viewers on a ride-along in the Bronx with one of New York's busiest companies, Engine 48. The sixty-five Bronx fire stations get about 160,000 alarms a year, however, they are nowhere near as busy as they were in the 70's and 80's, when at times Bronx companies would go from fire to fire, and hardly see their station during their whole tour. The program highlights arson investigations, fire rescues, and explanations of firefighting techniques. Produced by Tony Comiti for VM Productions and Monarch, the twenty-six minute documentary is offered in syndication by American Public Television.

Fire On the Mountain on the History Channel aired November 2002. Based on Chicago Tribune reporter John Maclean's acclaimed 1999 book of the same name. On July 6, 1994, a raging fire on Storm King Mountain in Colorado chased firefighters up a slope where they were overrun and died. Official reports blamed the deaths on the fourteen elite firefighters who lost their lives. John Maclean refused to believe that. His extensive investigation into the tragedy found many causes which included an understaffed and underpaid group of public servants not able to defend land and people from the blazing enemy. The documentary interviews the SmokeJumpers who were there, Federal investigators who refused to sign the official report, and family members of the victims. Scott Glenn narrates.

Engine Company X is the working title of a docmentary film that looks at the contributions and sacrifices made by African-Americans who have served, are currently serving, and will serve with two of the nation's premiere fire departments: the Los Angeles City and the Los Angeles County Fire Departments. It will also look at an organization that has exisxted within the two for decades, 'The Stentorians'. Still in the development stages, writer, producer and director Chin Thammasaengsri says that the project is divided into three sections: The Past, The Present, and The Future.

In The Past, stories and experiences told by those firemen who lived them is the main thrust of the documentary. At the forefront of the early struggle for integration in the Los Angeles City Fire Department was a group who eventually took the name "Stentorians." "These men stood up against a system determined to segregate them into two Los Angeles City Fire Stations using non-violence. They were subjected to the infamous "Hate Houses" where they experienced a wide range of personal indignities," states Chin. The documentary goes on to record how the group now known as the "Old Stentorians" stood firm and forced the leadership of the department to make the change. That change came in

1954, when the City of Los Angeles integrated all city firehouses. The stories these men told threaten to be lost in the sands of time as they slowly pass on, so the Westlake Signal Group (WSG) is working feverishly to record them for The Stentorians and the world at large.

A historical timeline (predating the formation of The Stentorians) is told by "Old" Stentorian and Griot, Arnett Hartsfield. Hartsfield, a lawyer and a firefighter, drafted many complaints handed to the LAFD and was instrumental in holding the line between ever-present specters of violence that threatened to erupt as tensions flared. Hartsfield recounts on film the history of Blacks on the LAFD beginning with the arrival of the first one in 1897 through 1961 when Hartsfield left the department to continue his career in law.

Los Angeles County's history with African-Americans begins in 1957 when the first Black is hired. The difference between L.A. City and County is that the County Fire Department never experienced segregation, but, as it was termed, they experienced "isolation" in county stations where they were ignored and made to otherwise feel unwanted. Los Angeles County's history is represented by Stentorian and current Los Angeles County Fire Captain Brent Burton who also serves the group as its Griot as well. Chin also interviews from L.A. County Assistant Chief Hershel Clady, and retired L.A. City Firefighter Keith Kenworthy, a white firefighter, who experienced the 'fires of hate' when he stood against segregation.

During the course of producing the documentary, cameras will go out into the field and look how today's Los Angeles City and County Fire Departments are different from the one the old Stentorians came into. WSG cameras wll ride with Engine and Task Force Companies as they respond to emergency calls and roll with Battalion Chiefs, PIO's, and other fire department personnel as they perform their day-to-day duties. All the while WSG will attempt to get the firefighters' perspective on the job today and how it differs from the world of the 1950's. "Preserving the past for the future is a very large job", states Chin, "especially for The Stentorian organization." Cameras have already recorded members of the Stentorians who run a training program designed to prepare young people of all backgrounds for entrance into the fire service. WSG will be filming at the James Shern Fire Academmy in Compton and recording the training sessions held there. Interviews with young "hopefuls" will give the viewer an insight into the effects the sacrfices made long before they were born have affected them and their dreams of going into this most noble profession.

Chin advised that the planned premier for this project would be at the IABPFF Convention (International Association of Black Professional Firefighters), which will be held in Los Angeles in 2004. The two hour piece will then run as a permanent exhibit at the African-Americna Firefighter Museum at 1401 S. Central Avenue in Los Angeles. The many hours of rough footage compiled by WSG will be donated to The Stentorian organization for their permanent historical archives.

WSG's future plans for the project will include seeking interest by broadcast entities such as the History Channel or Biography in addition to the film competition circuit. *Engine Company X* Executive Producer, Writer, and Director is Chin Thammasaengsri. Produced by Andrea Beckum and Jesus Sanchez for the Weslake Signal Group. Host Narrator: Calvin Walton. WSG's previous project was another firefighter themed drama entitlled *"The C-Shift"* previously mentioned.

Along the same theme, but featurng the San Diego Fire Department is **The Men of Station 19**. It is the story of the first African-American firefighters in the San Diego Fire Department. The program starts with the first two that were hired in 1919 through present day, where 35% of the force is made up of people of color and women. The Emmy winning eight minute feature, first aired on San Diego's KPBS in February 2001. The documentary film interviews several now retired and current firefighters and told the story of segregation and integration in the San Diego Fire Department. Station 19 was known as San Diego's 'Black Fire Station' as that is where all Black firefighters were sent. Only a specific number of Black firefighters could be hired at that time, as one would have to leave the fire service before another could be hired.

Even through the 40's and 50's as more African-Americans were hired and sent to other stations in the city, they told of how they handled the hostility and isolation by 'doing their job'. As such they don't consider themselves pioneers or heroes.

Fire Station 19 is no longer an active firehouse. It is now owned by the Brothers United and has their offices and a small amount of memorabilia pertaining to their early years in the Fire Department. Robert Osby, who was one of the founding members of the Brothers United in 1972, would eventually become Chief of the Deparment in 1992. The new Station 19, just a few blocks from the original, has a plaque mounted on the station honoring those early firefighters. San Diego's Deputy Mayor Stevens, in commending the Black firefighters of Station 19 for their contributions to the City of San Diego proclaimed June 3, 2002 to be "The Men of Station 19 Day" in the City of San Diego by resolution R-2002-1503. *The Men of Station 19* was written and produced by Jim Holzman for Broadcast Images, Inc. Creator and Executive Producer is Russell Steppe, Engineer SDFD. The program continues to air on KPBS stations.

CHAPTER TWELVE —
DIARY OF AN ARSONIST

Okay, so why is this chapter here, you ask? I'll explain; during the 1980's and early 1990's, Southern California was plagued by a series of mysterious fires. The arsonist's lethal handiwork led to the death of four people, and millions of dollars worth of property damage, which included homes, retail stores, and fields of dry brush during the hot summer months.

He could be described as a "wolf in sheep's clothing," hiding in plain sight–undetected for years. US Government profilers describe him as "probably one of the most prolific American arsonists of the 20th Century." He has been the subject of numerous interviews and documentaries since his arrest, including *Inside Edition, NOVA, Arrest & Trial, Investigative Reports*, TV news magazines, and *Court TV* as late as June 2002. I am speaking of former Glendale California Fire Department's fire investigator, John Orr, who was arrested in December of 1991, tried and convicted, and is now serving four life sentences + 12 years for a total of twenty-six counts of arson, and four counts of murder.

He was one of the most respected and sought-after arson investigators in the state. He was an instructor at arson investigation seminars (I even attended his classes), training sessions, and a writer of manuals and articles in trade magazines. He often assisted nearby agencies in solving their "origin and cause" of arson fires, some of which, after arriving on scene, he would immediately identify the point of origin of the fire.

I include convicted arsonist and murderer John Orr's story here, not to give him credit, but to note his television appearances, and more. The latest was in June 2002, when *Court TV* aired a documentary program *The Firestarter - John Orr* (the interview took place the Summer of 2001), where he vehemently denies any guilt for the acts for which he was convicted, including the three counts to which he pleaded guilty in a plea bargain.

John Orr authored a book, *Points of Origin*, which he began writing in early 1990. It is said that it reads more like a diary than a fact-based fictional novel, which was used by the prosecutors during the trial. In 1992, Orr sold the rights to his book, completed in April 1991, to HBO and received a retainer of $1,500, with the balance of $15,000 to follow if it were ever produced. Ten years later HBO presented *Point of Origin*, a ninety-minute TV movie, which aired during the later part of June 2002, starring Ray Liotta as John Orr.

HBO's release states, "Based on a true story, this twisting psychological thriller focuses on a serial arsonist, whose terrifying six-year crime spree is juxtaposed with the increasingly desperate efforts of investigators to bring him to justice. Charged with investigating many of these fires is Captain John Orr (Ray Liotta), a legendary figure in the Glendale Fire Department, possessed with an uncanny ability to pinpoint the origins of a fire, as well as the devices by which an arsonist may have carried out the crime. Through a fingerprint left at the scene of one crime and a series of surprise revelations focusing on arsons set in several towns, the task force is able to close in on an unlikely suspect... and ultimately crack the case."

Now you can read *Points of Origin*, the manuscript confiscated from John Orr's home at the time of his arrest, published by Infinity Publishing Company in Pennsylvania.

Returning to print after a six-year hiatus, former LAPD detective sergeant and best selling author, Joseph Wambaugh, focuses on firefighters rather than his usual police beat, probing into the life of arson investigator John Leonard Orr. Joseph Wambaugh (*The*

Onion Field) published *The Fire Lover: A True Story,* released in June 2002. Probing through court records and interviews of all the major principals involved, Wambaugh gives a never-before released account of many of the fires set, and the surveillance of Orr through the arrest and trial. The book also includes editorial review from *Publishers Weekly.*

Per California law, neither John L. Orr nor his family will profit from the sale of Orr's book. A restitution fund has been set up with the State of California Victim Compensation Program, and an agreed upon percentage of sales will go into that fund. John Orr will not and cannot profit from any of the money made from these endeavors, including the making of the movie from his book.

CHAPTER THIRTEEN —
9/11-RELATED DOCUMENTARIES

After the devastating attack in New York, Washington DC, and Pennsylvania on September 11, 2001, many videos and TV documentaries chronicling the heroic efforts of the men and women, both in the public service and civilian sector, have been produced. They have primarily focused on New York where so many lives were lost.

Not much has been filmed or aired of the attack on the Pentagon where one hundred eighty-nine people died, including those on the plane and the ground. Two Pentagon firefighters suffered serious second-degree burns, as they took cover behind their new fire truck, which was destroyed, as the plane dove into the Pentagon. In Pennsylvania, forty-four lives were lost, all from the aircraft, when it crashed into the Pennsylvania countryside.

The following are just some of the documentaries that have been made. More are sure to follow in the days and months ahead.

On the CBS news program *48 Hours*, which aired December 14, 2001, Dan Rather hosts ***A Company of Heroes***, which profiles a new breed of American hero. They follow the men of FDNY's Rescue 1, as they save lives, and ultimately lose eleven of their own. With footage shot one month before the World Trade Center attack, correspondent Bill Lagattuta, using footage shot for *The Bravest* features some of Rescue 1's most dramatic rescues. The surviving members of Rescue 1 tell correspondent Lagattuta about the struggle to continue saving lives, while coping with their own loss and grief. They made weekly trips to Ground Zero to aid in recovery efforts, and unflinchingly perform their daily rescues. In the end, they say that's how they will carry on: "I think we're the luckiest people on the planet, despite what happened, because we get to make a difference every day," says firefighter Paul Hashagen. "One of the things about firefighters is they're not heroes because they died. They're heroes because of what they do every day," he adds. Tom Forman, Joe Halderman, and Josh Gelman produced. Associate Producers were Hillary Tullin, Nomi Ernst, and Ian Paisley. Reid Collins, Jr. was Senior Producer; Hal Gessner was Executive Editor, and Susan Zirinsky was Executive Producer.

Tales from Ground Zero premiered on the Animal Planet on December 17, 2001. It shared the stories of our four-legged companions, and their experiences during and after the September 11 disaster. The hour-long special featured several tales (pun intended) of a man saved from the World Trade Center by his seeing-eye dog, an owner's search for her pet pug after they were separated by the post-collapse devastation, a rescue dog doing his job inside Ground Zero, a cat who birthed kittens at Ground Zero, and a pack of friendly pups helping to heal those experiencing emotional pain.

BNNtv.com produced *Tales from Ground Zero* in association with Animal Planet. Steve Rosenbaum, Executive Producer for BNNtv.com, commented thus; "From therapy dogs helping at memorial services, and K9 dogs working in the piles of rubble, animals were an essential part of the rescue and recovery effort."

BNNtv has also produced *America 911* on home video, as a memorial and remembrance of the World Trade Center Tragedy. The seventy-minute video contains footage of the first twenty-four hours after the disaster, the unbelievable heroism and determination of those first hours, and features on the aftermath. *America 911* is intended as a tribute and a memorial to the fallen, and a permanent reminder lest we ever forget. A portion of the proceeds from the sale of each video is being donated to the American Red Cross Disaster Relief Fund.

Also from BNNtv is Producer Steve Rosenbaum's *7 Days in September,* from Camera Planet Pictures. The video depicts first person accounts by twenty-seven New Yorkers in the first week following 9/11. The project is still being worked on at this writing. It is proposed to be at least a thirty-minute documentary.

9-11-01: The World Trade Center - Day of Disaster, a sixty-minute video by FDNY photographer, Steve Spak, was filmed shortly after the collapse of the Twin Towers. This video will take you on Spak's journey through the ruins of the World Trade Center; you'll see the fires that were burning, and hear fire ground radio transmissions. "I think this video is an important part of our history! We must NEVER FORGET the victims of this awful tragedy!" says Spak. Spak, a freelance photographer for more than twenty-five years donates his photos and videos to the FDNY for training purposes. Former Fire Commissioner, Thomas Von Essen, honored him on June 16th 2001 when he was promoted to the rank of Honorary Deputy Chief. The video is available at fdnyphoto.com.

Presented as an official selection at the 2002 Sundance Film Festival was *WTC: The First 24 Hours*. The film was shot over a twenty-four hour period, from the morning of September 11, 2001 to the morning of September 12. There are two versions of the film, an eleven-minute short, seen at Sundance, and a thirty-minute documentary. The video has no narration or music; the only sound is ambient natural sound such as sirens, wind blowing, machinery, radio transmissions, muffled voices, and explosions. Selected images will be seen in a later CBS documentary titled *9/11*. The film was produced, directed, and filmed by Etienne Sauret. The thirty-minute documentary has also been presented at the New York Historical Society, and premiered September 2002 on HBO.

New York Firefighters: The Brotherhood of September 11 premiered on the Discovery Channel on March 8 2002. This documentary focused on Rescue 3, those that died and those that survived. Out of the three hundred forty-three New York firefighters who died on Sept. 11, eight came from Rescue 3. Of the eight that died, Captain Brian Hickey of Rescue 4 just happened to be on Rescue 3 that day on an overtime shift. Filmed in October 2001, the surviving members of the firehouse, including the wives and children, opened up their lives to the Discovery Channel. The documentary was narrated by Stockard Channing, and produced by Partisan Pictures. Filmmaker Peter Schnall knew the firefighters and was invited to film at Rescue 3.

Starting with the brief image, ten seconds is all viewers saw of a firefighter, and then the camera panned up to a plane, the first plane, slamming into the World Trade Center building is only the beginning of an as yet untitled video. Jules Naudet, a twenty-eight year-old Paris-born filmmaker, was filming a documentary of a probationary firefighter, Tony Benetatos, the filming of which had begun some months earlier at Engine Co. 7 - Ladder 1. That fateful morning, before a shift change near the World Trade Center, he captured the horrific image. Millions watched as the plane crashed into the North Tower, and with cameras in hand, Jules and his brother rushed toward the WTC, along with firefighters, police, and emergency teams. The rest of Naudet's video captures firefighters in the WTC lobby, commanders setting up a command post, the evacuation when the second plane hit, and the collapse of the South Tower, but most of all, it captured the faces of those who died that day; the last brave actions of the firefighters, Port Authority officers, and civilians. About ninety firefighters that died have been identified on his tape.

According to FDNY spokesman, Francis X. Gribbon, officials have a copy of the tape, which will be partly investigative, and partly an historical artifact. A few copies of the tape have made the rounds of some New York firehouses. Jules Naudet, who along with his brother Gedeon, remained at the scene shooting five hours of video nearly died during the collapse of the North Tower, and only barely made it out. The video was seen in the UK on London's Channel 4 on Jan 30, 2002.

CBS Television reportedly paid the Naudet brothers $2 million dollars for the rights to broadcast a two-hour documentary special titled *9/11*, hosted by New Yorker and two-time Oscar winner, Robert DeNiro, in the US on March 10, 2002. FDNY firefighter James Hanlon from Ladder 1, a friend of the Naudet brothers, acted as Technical Advisor to assist the producers and editors at CBS News during the re-editing process, and is also the program's narrator. The documentary is a narrative of the experience of one firehouse and its men–in the weeks before Sept. 11, to the rescue operation at Ground Zero, to the funeral of a fellow firefighter. Senior Broadcast Producer and writer for CBS is Tom Fontana (*Philly Heat, Family Brood, Firehouse*) for Goldfish Pictures Inc., and Silverstar Productions.

Six months later, Tony (badge number 3865) is now working Haz Mat 1, stationed in Queens (Haz Mat 1 shares quarters with Squad 288). As of the airing of *9/11* in March 2002, less than half of the three hundred forty-three NY personnel lost had been recovered.

A global broadcast of *9/11* will air primarily on PBS, and other worldwide public broadcast stations on the first anniversary of the attack. A spokesman for the Naudet brothers stated that they hoped it would reach approximately 80% of the world's viewers.

On September 12, 2002, Paramount Home Video released CBS's *9/11: Filmmaker edition;* a one hundred thirty-minute extended version in letterbox format, with added interviews, which is also available in DVD.

Tom Downey, documentary filmmaker and son of a New York firefighter produced, **Rescue Company, New York City**. During 2001, Tom Downey rode with New York's elite Rescue 1 and Rescue 2.

The filmmaker's uncle and cousins are Rescue firefighters. Fire Chief, Ray Downey, commanded all the Rescue companies, and Capt. Joe Downey and Lt. Chuck Downey are rescue firefighters in their father's special operations command. When the towers fell on September 11th, Chief Downey led the evacuation. His sons searched the rubble daily. "One of us is there every day," they said. Chief Downey's remains were discovered mid May 2002, and his funeral service was held May 20, 2002. Downey was the one hundred eighty-ninth FDNY official to be recovered from the WTC site, as well as the last, leaving one hundred fifty-four not found. CBS News Correspondent, Scott Pelley, reports the documentary will air later in 2002 on TLC.

The MSNBC cable channel presented *24 Hours at Ground Zero*, an inside look at the first twenty-four hours of the WTC disaster, through the eyes of a firefighter, a police officer, and an EMS worker, who were among the first to arrive on the scene. The documentary begins with the attacks on the towers, focuses on the Search and Rescue effort, and then ends with the sun rising over New York the following morning.

Why the Towers Fell? was produced by the acclaimed NOVA series, and presented by BBC/WGBH for Public Broadcasting (PBS) on April 30, 2002. Utilizing parts of the Naudet brothers' now famous film, it follows a team of forensic engineers through their investigation of the Twin Towers' collapse. This includes a series of animations of the planes approaching and striking the buildings, and the resulting fire and collapse.

The program also features an interview with Brian Clark, who worked on the eighty-fourth floor of Tower Two World Trade Center, and was one of only four to escape either tower from above the points of impact. He was also happened the fire marshal for his floor. Also interviewed was Leslie Robertson, the builder of the towers, who was only thirty-four years old at the time.

The program shows how several FDNY firefighters from Engine 6 remember their ordeal, and survived inside Tower One (the North tower with the antenna on top) after the collapse. They were in a third or fourth floor stairwell, and after the collapse they looked up to see the sky above their heads. Dr. Thomas Eagar, a professor of engineering at MIT, explains how their part of the stairwell survived the force of the falling 500,000-ton building, and protected the firefighters inside.

NOVA Producer, Larry Klein, who watched the investigators scour the debris for clues about the collapse, marveled at how they made sense of the twisted wreckage. In a written statement he said, "Like good crime detectives, these engineers came to the scene knowing what to look for, and over the next several months they found all the evidence they needed. The NOVA program I helped produce will be the first official public presentation of the results of this unprecedented investigation." The investigation by the American Society of Civil Engineers was commissioned by the Federal Emergency Management Agency, and the fully written report, called a Building Performance Study, was released May 1, 2002.

In Memoriam: New York City, 9/11/01 debuted Memorial Day weekend, Sunday, May 26 2002, exclusively on HBO. In December 2001, HBO's documentary division began work on a film chronicling the events of Sept. 11. It issued a call to the public for visual and audio contributions to the special. Families and individuals were invited to participate in the making of the documentary by contributing items such as photographs, home videos, voice mails, recollections, eyewitness accounts, and memories of loved ones.

HBO received about eight hundred hours of film, and ultimately used footage from sixteen news organizations, and more than one hundred fifteen individual videographers and photographers. This documentary provides a historical record of the tragic events of

September 11, 2001, through a personal collection of video and still photographs, shot by more than one hundred people in and around New York City. The film follows the Honorable Mayor Rudolph W. Giuliani, and his senior staff from their first realization of the tragedy that had occurred.

Included is the work of Steve Spak, an honorary Deputy Chief of the New York City Fire Department, who works as an associate court clerk in Brooklyn. He was at home in Queens with his family on Sept. 11. Spak arrived on the scene just after the collapse of both towers. "It looked like hell on earth," he recalls. "It was what I didn't see that was the worst, I didn't see any survivors. Someone could have told me that I was on the moon, and I would have believed him." Spak has produced his own video on the WTC aftermath previously mentioned in this chapter.

On September 10th 2002, ABC aired a two-hour documentary, ***Report from Ground Zero***, based on former New York firefighter, Dennis Smith's best selling book. In their own words, it chronicles the actions and events of New York's first responders – police officers, firefighters, EMS personnel, and Port Authority officers. Original footage of Ground Zero, and the construction to the World Trade Center complex is also shown.

Report from Ground Zero was published on March 18th 2002. It is story of the rescue-and-recovery operations at the World Trade Center during the days that followed September 11th 2001, through the eyes of New York firefighters and others. (See: dennissmith.com). Dennis had another one of his books made into a documentary, *Report from Engine Co. 82*, which was be discussed in an earlier chapter.

...September 11, 2002...a year later. Memorial services were held not only across the nation, but also around the world. Tributes and a reading of the names lost at ground zero, moments of silence at places of work, prayers for those that are gone, but not forgotten. Worldwide, for most of the day, documentaries aired over the networks.

Cast of *Police Rescue*. L-R: John Clayton as Inspector Bill Adams, Belinda Cotterill as Sharyn Elliot, Steve Bisley as Kevin 'Nipper' Harris, Gary Sweet as Steve 'Mickey' McClintock, Sonia Todd as Georgia Rattray, Steve Bastoni as Yionnis 'Angel' Angelopoulous, Tammy McIntosh as Kathy Orland, and Jeremy Callaghan as Brian Morley.
Photo by ABC (Austrailian Broadcasting Co.)

CHAPTER FOURTEEN — INTERNATIONAL TV FIREFIGHTERS

AUSTRALIA

Police-Rescue, set in Sydney, Australia, aired from 1990-1996, and was produced with the full cooperation of the New South Wales Police Department, which included total script approval. The program was based on a real division of the NSW Police Dept., which was established in 1942 as a "Cliff Rescue Squad."

I include this program, as it is more like a fire or EMS program than a police drama. The program is much like *Rescue 8* and *Emergency!* There are several two-person crews in the drama series, which operate their specially equipped Nissan and Toyota Rescue vehicles out of a station house. The two-story facility houses the dispatch center, maintenance, dorm, shower, and kitchen areas.

They perform all the vehicle accident rescues, confined space rescues, Hi-Rise rescues, and a variety of other situations all with their specialized gear such as Hydraulic equipment, SCBA's, metal detectors, vertical rope rescue equipment, and more that would typically be done in the States by the fire department. The rescue crews don't wear side arms, except for the Senior Sergeant. They work with the Sydney Fire Brigade on occasion. Southern Star Xanadu and the Australian Broadcasting Network (ABC) are the co-production companies of *Police-Rescue*. The series was filmed all around Sydney, as well as along the resort area of the Central Coast and spectacular Blue Mountains. The program is currently in syndication.

"When its 1000 degrees Celsius (1832F) inside, and everyone else is running out…they go running in." This is the premise behind Australia's *Fire*, "A stunning one hour drama series about the last, real action heroes – firefighters." After two years of research by the producers, an ongoing one-hour firefighting drama series premiered on the Seven Network in February 1995, and aired two seasons through 1996 with a total of twenty-six episodes.

Filmed in the coastal city of Brisbane in Queensland, the storylines were all based on real people and events. The series featured the eight-member crew of a fictitious fire station in Brisbane, the South-East Station, and the events were based on the exploits of the Carlton Fire Station (in Melbourne) in the 1980's. The first season's storyline was based on a series of arsons, in actuality a school kid, but for the series a firefighter was depicted as the arsonist.

At seasons end, when the Pyromaniac was revealed to be a member of the crew, the station drew a 48% share of the household's watching, nearly half of the TV viewing population of the country. The first episode briefly featured full-frontal nudity of a male firefighter, as he attempted to intimidate the new female recruit in an incident of sexual harassment, which causes division and strife within the fire station. She is the first woman to join the "firies" as they are called in Australia. There were no females in the "real" Brisbane Fire Service at the time. The second season's drama, which was "more raunchy," according to producer Tony Cavanaugh, had female nudity as well. Season two developed into three different continuing storylines, again, all based on actual incidents.

Some of the firefighters nicknames were quite catchy, such as, "Repo," "Spit," "Nick the Boss," "Dinosaur," "TNT," and "Mad Dog," as the first female firefighter hired in Brisbane. Georgie Parker, a three-time Australian *TV Week Silver Logie Award* winner, as "Mad Dog" says about *Fire*, "It was vile! It was the most unglamorous shoot I've done in my life...we all looked like s_ _ _!"

TV Firefighters

Scene from Austrailia's "Fire"
Photo courtesy of Beyond International LTD

Although the intent was to film in Melbourne, the show was relocated to Brisbane, and initially had the full support of the Queensland Fire and Rescue Service. They, their representatives, and the firefighters union read and commented on all the scripts, and were always on hand to ensure safe (for the actors) firefighting scenes. Prior to filming, the actors attended a rigorous two-week training session. The series took five months to shoot. Fire equipment was rented from the Fire Service for the first season.

Support for the series, although granted by the Fire Service, was withdrawn prior to filming season two due to the firefighters union objections, when it was evident that actions by the characters violated HMR and Queensland Fire Service Policies. Like *LA Firefighters* in the States, ironically enough in the same year, the second season saw a name change from representing the Queensland Fire Service to the fictitious Queensland Fire Brigade. Uniform and logo changes were also made, and the production company had to purchase two engines for the series. A new station location was required, so they were "transferred" to the

West-End Station. "We actually built our fire stations, complete with pole! We revamped the outsides — they were empty factories, brick, built many years ago. Both have been demolished since. We did film in and around real fire stations on numerous occasions (in the first series), and had real firies and their BRT's (Big Red Trucks) in the action. The real firies were hired as special extras," states Cavanaugh.

The Queensland Fire Service Technical Advisors doubled as firefighters in some scenes. The engine used in season one was a new Firepac FP4000 manufactured by Austral Specialized Vehicles of Brisbane, Australia. The company went out of business in 1999, but still have several vehicles in service throughout the country. The Firepac continues to be manufactured by another company called Varley Engineering in Australia. Also utilized in the series was a Telescopic Aerial Platform on an International 1900 series chassis. One of the second season's engines (purchased by the company) was an ex-South Australian Metropolitan Fire Service unit - a 1973 RFW/Wormald/Simon SS85 snorkel (Robert F. Whithead, Australian specialist manufacturer of all wheel drive vehicles. Wormald built bodies for fire apparatus, mainly in New Zealand, and is no longer in business.)

"Fire" Engine used in season one, one of only 10 manufactured by A.S.V.
Photo by Dr. Steven Schueler

Fire is still airing in syndication in several countries around the world, but not in the US as "most Australian shows are a little challenging for the US market due to the accents," according to Cavanaugh. The show was conceived and produced by Liberty Films in association with Beyond Productions for the Seven Network. *Fire* co-creator, writer, and producers are Tony Cavanaugh, with Michael Caulfield and Simone North for the Brisbane based Liberty & Beyond Pty. Ltd. Tony Cavanaugh states, "We are very proud of our show, and feel it is a great reflection, warts and all, of life in the service."

Emergency 000 is a documentary produced in Australia, also by the Liberty and Beyond Company, with the full cooperation of the Emergency Services. Airing in 1996 and 1997, the thirteen episodes (per season) followed the Australian Emergency Service crews (ambulance, fire, and police) in their daily work. The stories were not recreations, but were told on the spot by the actual participants. The program is still airing in syndication in Australia and on Reality TV. It will soon air in the Asian-Pacific region as well, via ABC (Australia Broadcasting Co) Asian-Pacific Network. (000 is Australia's equivalent of America's 911).

CANADA
The Forest Rangers was reportedly one of the most successful Canadian series in CBC history. In fact, it was the first Canadian TV series to be made in color. It aired from 1964 through 1966 with one hundred and four, thirty-minute programs, and was distributed to forty countries worldwide, including the US. It chronicled the adventures of Chief Ranger George Keeley, played by Graydon Gould, and his crew of five Junior Forest Rangers in the mythical town of Indian River, somewhere in Northern Canada. The program featured the Canadian, British, Indian, and French people working together reporting forest fires and other crimes. Many of the ideas for the show came from authentic stories. Filming took place on location, and at the Toronto International Studios, north of

the village of Kleinburg, located today in the City of Vaughan, for the Canadian Broadcasting Corp, and the Incorporated Television Co., UK. Produced by ASP and Maxine Samuels, who was the show's creator and Executive Producer. *Les Cadets de la forêt* is the French title. This "kids and family" oriented show is currently in syndication on a Canadian cable network. The kids were often seen wearing Smokey Bear sweatshirts, and flying a Smokey Bear flag at their campground.

The Forest Rangers (Canadian) L-R: Peter Tully, Ronald Cohoon, Ralph Endersby, Susan Conway, Graydon Gold as the Chief Ranger Keeley, and George Allen. Photo by CBC (Canadian Broadcasting Co.)

In the Line of Duty was another of the dramatic fly-on-the-wall series where cameramen lived in the Firehalls, and would go along to each call. Cameras followed the work of firefighters, paramedics, police, and rescue workers. Everything was real, and nothing recreated. Segments included firefighters battling blazes, paramedics saving lives on the streets, emergency response teams dealing with hostage situations, search and rescue squads locating missing persons, and specially-trained personnel handling the dangers posed by hazardous materials. This thirty-five episode series was produced and filmed solely in Vancouver, Canada, and featured "ride-a-long" footage with various fire companies. This Canadian reality series was produced between 1995 and 1997, and distributed by Forrer Communications; the Executive Producer of the program is Dan Forrer. It is still in syndication in several countries.

TV Firefighters

Presented by Radio-Canada *Caserne 24* (*Firehouse 24*) was a realistic, high drama action series about the world of firefighting, which aired on Wednesday nights at 7:30pm. The series first aired on September 16, 1998, and ran three seasons through April 2001 with eighty-eight episodes, but was only shown in the French-speaking provinces, as it was not subtitled into English. According to producers, "Chief Albert Chabot and his team of firefighters work at Station 24. They share everything: not only do they face the worst together; they also eat, bunk, and party together. Although they're well-trained and well-equipped to deal with difficult conditions, they can also at times be helpless and awkward when they have to confront personal issues. No matter what the situation, however, they never lose their sense of humor-these brave firefighters are, above all, good and decent men."

Cast of
Caserne 24
Photo by Sovimage
Production Co.

The thirty-minute programs were filmed in and around Montreal, and produced by Les Productions Sovimage in Quebec. There was a close collaboration between the producers and the Fire Prevention Service of the City of Montreal, to guarantee the accuracy of firefighting scenes and ensure realism. The series was filmed in a real (out of service) fire station, formerly old station 45, at 4200 East

Ontario Street, Montréal (Québec). The actors all went through training at a firefighters' school, to become proficient in the handling of equipment. The popular program garnered a 39% market share of the viewers during its run. It is still being aired in syndication.

Jacques Payette (season one) and Claudette Viau (seasons two and three) produced the program; Claudette Viau was Executive Producer for the Sovimage Production Company, and Jean Bourbonnais and François Côté directed. The fire equipment used during the first and third season were demo units provided by Superior Emergency Vehicles Ltd. (Superior E-One) of Alberta Canada. During the first season they ran with a new E-1 Cyclone TC series, Cross Mount Panel, and the Cyclone 2TC series side panel during the third season. After the series ended, the engines were sold to the City of Oshawa, Ontario, and to Ville de Saint Jerome, Quebec respectively. Other equipment utilized was a 1994 Spartan Nova 100 foot Quintech, as Aerial 424 now in service in Montreal as Ladder 429 at Station 29, and a privately owned 1966 Mack pumper. Repeat episodes continue to be aired.

Cyclone 2TC side mount Photo by Superior E-One in Alberta, Canada

Fire Station was a 13-part thirty-minute docu-soap series, which aired on Canada's Discovery Channel. Co-Executive Producers, Anne Pick, and Ina Fichman and their team spent three months beginning October 2000 playing "fly on the wall" at Toronto's second-largest station, Clermont Hall, which has a roster of fifty-seven firefighters, including one woman. They are also among the cities busiest; in January 2001 they answered two hundred ninety-six calls.

The 1.2 million dollar series features the close bonds that form around the firehouse, and the horrors to which they are exposed. The hours are long, the pay mediocre, the danger great, yet despite all of this, most firefighters will tell you there's no life like it. "It's just they're the white knights," theorizes Pick. "Firemen, all they do is come rescue you and look after your needs, whether it's medical, whether it's reassurance, or to get your cat out of the tree, they're happy to help. What more could you want? Here's a hero who risks his life, and cooks and cleans." Productions La Fête & Wombat Productions produced, in association with the Discovery Channel, Canal Z, and WTN-Women's Television Network. Original episodes aired February through June 2001.

CHINA
Burning Flame (*Lit Fo Hung Sam* - Chinese title translates to *Flaming Passion*).

The drama is about three firefighters called the "Nam Shan Three Tigers" (named after their housing estates), in a fire station in Hong Kong, China, their undying friendship to each other, the test of both love and work, and their fight against a maniac arsonist. The fire station used in the series was a five-bay station; a fireboat and motorcycles are also utilized. Fire apparatus used were 1980's Carmichael / Dennis RS engines. The cast also included two female firefighters. Airing Monday through Friday evenings, the series began October 12, 1998, and ran through December 6, 1998, airing forty-one episodes; a popular program as it garnered an 81 % audience share rating. The series was awarded Best Drama Program at the 1999 Asian Television Festival, and placed fourth at the 1999 Nextmedia Awards ~ Top Ten TV Programs.

Burning Flame II
Advertising
Poster

A new series began production in May 2001 with a slight title change to ***Burning Flame II,*** and completed shooting in December. This new thirty-five episode series premiered in Hong Kong on July 29, 2002. *BFII* is not a sequel, and has a new plot with a new cast and new characters. Executive Producer for both series is Ms. Amy Wong Sun-Wai. The series is a Wong Sun-Wai production by Television Broadcasts Limited (TVB) TV City, Kowloon, Hong Kong. Both series were produced with the assistance and full support of the Hong Kong Fire Services Department, and with the Fire Brigade's PLG (Public Liaison Group). The

TV Firefighters 167

Kowloon Fire Services Department is often on hand to view the shooting. The series is seen in some select US markets (released in June 2002), and in Asian and Far East countries in the Cantonese language only.

ENGLAND

An early comedy program featuring firefighters was titled *Fire Crackers*. First airing August 29th 1964, it followed the misadventures of inept firemen in the Village of Croppers End, population seventy. The men at the fire station spent most of their time drinking at the local pub, *Croppers Arms*, playing cards, or sleeping. Once in a while the work-shy crew had no alternative but to go off and fight a fire in their antique 1907 Merryweather fire engine named "Bessie."

Fire Crackers advertisement

Created by Fred Robinson, the series ran two seasons, with thirteen thirty-minute black and white episodes airing on Saturday evenings at 9:30pm. Alfred Marks starred as "Charlie the Chief," John Arnett as Station Officer (Captain) Blazer, an appropriate firefighter name (who was actually born in Russia). Other unusual firefighter names were "Tadpole," "Hairpin," "Loverboy," and "Jumbo." Directed by Josephine Douglas and produced by Alan Tarrant for ATV – Associated Television [UK] (now ITV Network), the series was filmed at the ATV Studios in Elstree, north of London. The August 24, 1964 issue of UK's *TV Times* featured a cover photo and article about the program.

The Firefighters, a 1974 series aimed primarily at children, followed the adventures of the Grant children who lived near a fire station. They helped out with fire drills and other tasks. In one episode, they are accused of arson when a series of fires occur, and the children eventually unearth the real culprits. Another episode ends in a cliffhanger when two of the kids are trapped in a burning warehouse. Sharron Fussey, Vincent Hall, and sixteen-year-old Simon Gipps-Kent played the children. Glyn Owen and Anne Stallybrass play the parents. Richard Pennington wrote the series. It is unknown how many episodes were produced.

London's Burning, the longest running firefighting program in the world, concluded its fourteenth season in August 2002. It began in December 1986 with a $1,600,000 (USD) two-hour movie, written in 1985 by Jack Rosenthal, and attracted an audience of 12.5 million. His friendship with London firefighter Les Murphy, the husband of his au pair, inspired the movie. The script was triggered by riots in the North of London in 1985 at the Broadwater Farm, during which a police officer was murdered, and for the first time the London Fire Brigade came under actual attack.

TV Firefighters

London's Burning - Series 10
L-R: Steven Houghton, Richard Walsh, Clive Wood, Michael Garner, Andrew Kazamia, Zoe Heyes, Ben Onwukwe, Glen Murphy, John Alford
LWT Photo

In March 1988, the series debuted with most of the characters from the movie. Since then *London's Burning* has developed into one of the most successful home-grown drama series on British Television today. Rosenthal's writing contribution ended with the film, and there were only two scriptwriters that first season.

Airing at 9:00pm on Sundays on the ITV Network, *London's Burning* is known for its spectacular fires and rescues. A daring and dramatic Hi-Rise Rescue sequence was filmed in April 1999 on a retired British destroyer, the HMS Belfast (now a museum), docked just up stream from London's famous Tower Bridge. Also, in season twelve it was a Hi-Rise hotel fire that took not only the cast of *London's Burning*, but also an additional one hundred twenty "real" firefighters, and several days to shoot. The fire was so big and realistic that the LFB is considering using the footage to train their firefighters. Other season twelve statistics: they recreated an underground rescue in a tunnel under the Thames. The plot called for the tunnel to be flooded, only for the Thames to flood naturally it nearly created a real life disaster! The series consumed 10,000 gallons of kerosene, employed seven hundred off-duty firefighters, sank one luxury yacht, and crushed thirty cars.

Produced for London Weekend Television (LWT) with the full cooperation of the London Fire & Emergency Planning Authority, (London Fire Brigade) the sixty-minute program is based on actual Fire Brigade incidents. Producer Paul Knight states, "No matter how bizarre or dramatic, *London's Burning* is based on actual events taken from fire service reports, as we have access to their archive material." What comes to mind of course are the fires, vehicle extrications, rescues, and other major shouts (incidents) to be incorporated into the series. However, what may be the most unsuccessful animal rescue ever was even used. It took place on January 14, 1978, when volunteers from the British army were filling in for the striking firemen. (Yes, the public sector can strike in Britain). An elderly lady in South London called them to get her cat out of a tree. They extricated the cat with no difficulty whatsoever, and then ran it over as they drove back to the fire station. Amazing but true, and in fact used in an episode of the long-running program.

Starting with only six episodes in its first season, it reached eighteen episodes per series by season ten. Typically the seasons ran from November through March, with production resuming in April. The series may possibly be winding down, however, because seasons eleven to thirteen only had sixteen episodes per series, and the past two seasons premiere episodes have not started until January. Season fourteen, which began filming in November 2001, and did not begin airing until July 2002, will only have eight episodes airing through August 25th. The last episode is a two-hour movie/episode giving further fuel to the rumor that this will be the final season. Even though producer David Newcomb stated that this was not the case, it was announced in December 2002 that the crew of Blackwall attended its last shout. There was no usual cliffhanger in this last episode as it closed with the crew all standing outside watching a meteor shower.

Cast of
London's Burning
in their new "Inferno"
fire gear.
LWT Photo

With the revised shooting and airing schedule for season fourteen they have effectively skipped a season. There was a new creative team behind this series, and the show wanted to move from its "soft" Sunday spot to a weeknight slot after 9:00pm to allow it to show more graphic scenes than before. The move did not happen, and it still aired on Sundays, but with more graphic sexual scenes and partial nudity. New theme music was introduced, making this the third theme produced for the series.

Award-winning producer Paul Knight produced the movie, and seasons one through ten of the series. Beginning with Season 11, the series is produced by David Shanks, along with Angus Towler. David Newcomb came aboard for Seasons 12 to 14.

London's Burning centers on the drama and lives, both on and off the job, with continuing storylines, of the Blue Watch (shift) of a London fire station. Throughout the movie and series there has always been a female crewmember. The London Fire Brigade hired their first female firefighter in 1982, and only had six on duty when the movie debuted. During the series, four members of Blue Watch have been killed in the line of duty. Paul Knight stated, "I made a decision at the end of season two to kill off a member of the cast. The unlucky character was one of the most popular, and the audience could not believe at first we actually killed him off. It was exactly the reaction we wanted and it gave the series some of the edge we needed." In Season five one of Blackwall's engines was involved in a rollover, and the last episode of Season nine ended in a cliffhanger, with both of Blackwall's engines involved in another vehicle accident. Injured firefighters were waiting to be rescued with some of them lying unconscious.

Over forty members of Blue Watch have come and gone since its first airing in 1986, with only one member of the original cast still on duty at Blackwall. In the last episode of season thirteen, three characters left the show, and in the first episode of season fourteen, five members get 'axed' and are replaced by five new ones. One newcomer, Anthony Green, who trained at London's Suffolk station states, "People's views have definitely changed (since the World Trade Center disaster), the police and ambulance service have always been seen as doing a fantastic job, but the fire service was slightly separate from that. Firefighters do a great job, and we should never forget that."

The first twelve seasons and the movie were filmed at Dockhead (renamed Blackwall for the series), which is a three-bay fire station near the famous Tower Bridge on Mosley Street. Dockhead was (and still is) an operational station, which caused many retakes during the filming of the movie. The Production Company provided two portable buildings for the firefighters (the real ones) to live in, while the cast and crew of *London's Burning* took over the station. "It was a bit of a drag," according to one station officer, "but on the set catering kept everyone happy." The Dockhead firefighters performed all the firefighting sequences for the movie.

For the series, a full-scale reproduction of the upper floors, locker area, sleeping quarters, kitchen, etc, were constructed on a sound stage at the nearby Jacob Street Studios. For the 2001 season, they moved to a newer station in the city of Leyton in Northeast London (near the corner of Church Street and Oliver), but the station is still called Blackwall. One reason for the move was that the tourist traffic was reportedly becoming unbearable at Dockhead. They are currently using the Three Mills Studios near the new station, with all-new sets.

According to London's *Sun Times* of August 21, 2000, amazed firefighters were called to a blaze at the studio where *London's Burning* was being filmed. The fire, which destroyed paint and props, started in a warehouse where two workmen were using a grinder. A witness said: "The workmen tried to put out the fire with extinguishers, but eventually had to call out the real fire brigade. None of the *London's Burning* stars were around." (but I bet the workmen wished they had been). "When the professionals came along, they put it out within minutes." A London Fire Brigade spokesman said, "We were called out to deal with a fire at the studios in Bow, at around 5pm. It involved studios six and seven, and was put out quite quickly. It was not a big fire." A *London's Burning* spokeswoman said, "The cast are on holiday, and none was involved."

The two appliances (engines) used during the movie and first two seasons of the series were out of LFB's reserve fleet, and were manufactured by Shelvoke/SPV. They are currently in a museum in Waltham, England. LWT purchased two Dennis RS 133 engines, long a staple engine for the LFB, for use during the following seven seasons, and recently sold them for scrap. Since 1997, season ten's opener, engines "on the run" have been provided by the Saxon Fire Apparatus Company on a Volvo chassis. (A very nice riding engine I might add, from personal experience). For the 2001 season, new F16 Volvo/Saxons were utilized to go along with their new station. The Pump Ladder was a Volvo/Saxon-Sanbec, while the ALP

(Aerial Ladder Platform) was a Volvo/Saxon-Simon. The command vehicle was a Mercedes A Class vehicle, also new for this season. (The LFB currently run Mercedes 300T Wagons and E Class wagons for their officers, and not the A Class). In season fourteen, they replaced the ALP with another Volvo/Saxon Pump Ladder.

Station Officer Brian "Nobby" Clark of the LFB Press Office provided technical assistance, and acted as the set Safety Officer. Clark was given complete authority over whether a scene was safe to shoot, script approval, and to the technical accuracy of the program. (Something his US counterparts don't have the luxury of). Off-duty firefighters were utilized for the more hazardous scenes, and a standby fire crew is always in attendance. By season seven, Clark had retired from the LFB and Roger Kendall assumed the role of series Technical Advisor. In season fourteen, Roger Haite replaced Kendall. As usual, the life of a Fire Department Technical Advisor is not an easy one. Most of the criticism of the past series has been directed at Kendall, due to the lack of realism with which he supposedly let *London's Burning* film.

The firefighter hangout in the series, frequented in almost every episode, was a pub called the *Swan & Sugarloaf*, conveniently located around the corner from the fire station (Dockhead). In 1997, the pub was sold, and its new name, *The Ship Aground* was featured as such in the series. Starting with the thirteenth season, when the station locale moved, a new pub *The Oliver Twist* (actual

Saxon Fire apparatus on a Volvo chassis. This was used in Seasons 10 through 12 in *London's Burning*.

name), which is featured in the series is next door to Leyton (TV's Blackwall) fire station.

Besides new engines for the series, the *London's Burning* crew has kept time with the London Fire Brigade with new uniforms. They began the series with the traditional cork helmets, wool tunics, and yellow overtrousers, adopted in the 1970's. By 1991, they were wearing reflectorized Blue/Grey Nomex fire gear (turnouts/bunker gear), with a polycarbonite helmet. In 1999, the Fire Brigade and the cast of *London's Burning* were sporting the new Inferno fire gear manufactured by Lion Apparel, a US company.

Author in old style fire gear during training exercise at England's Fire Service College.

A Gallet-style helmet, manufactured by Cromwell, Model F650, is now being worn. All the fire gear and equipment used in the program by the actors is authentic and not lightweight props. The *London's Burning* team try to ensure that the situations you see, and the equipment used is as close to the real thing as possible. Blue Watch's fictional firefighters depict the kind of life-threatening situation where the right equipment is essential. The actors undergo a rigorous two-week training session, including ride-alongs at various stations, at the beginning of each season, at London's Fire Brigade Training Academy in Southwark. Series preparations and filming for the actors takes twelve to fifteen hours a day, six days a week. The seasons that aired eighteen episodes took nine months to prepare and shoot.

Jim Alexander in *London's Burning,* series 11 in blue/grey Nomex fire gear
LWT Photo

In 1986, *London's Burning* was nominated for Best Single Film, and in the Photography, Editing, and Makeup categories at the prestigious BAFTA Awards ceremony, but did not win in any category. *London's Burning* won the Royal Television Society Design

Award for Visual Effects in 1990 and 1997, in the "Craft and Design" category. Tom Harris, for special effects was the recipient. In 1992, the Television and Radio Industries Club named the show the ITV Program of the Year. The movie's creator and award-winning writer, Jack Rosenthal (he has not been involved in the series), was nominated for the British Academy Best Play (*London's Burning*) in 1997, and for BAFTA's Huw Wheldon Award in 1998. BAFTA (British Academy of Film and Television Arts) is the British version of the Oscars and Emmys combined. Since 1993, when the BFI began publishing the audience table, the British Film Institute (BFI) has continuously named *London's Burning* one of the Top 20 in Original Drama Production.

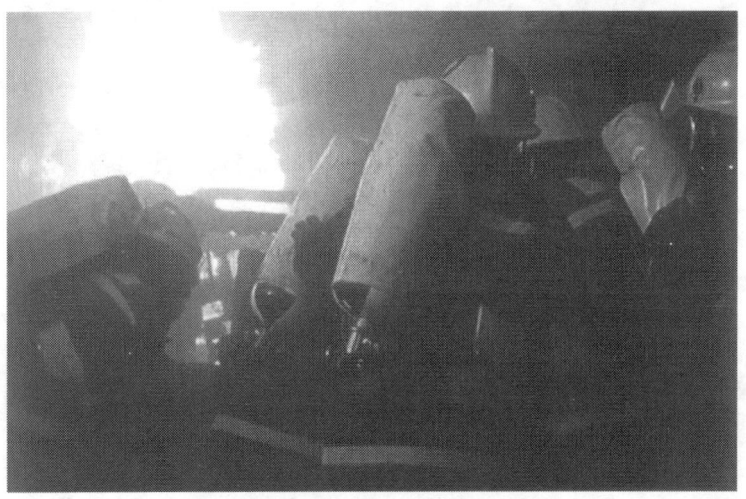

Fire scene from *London's Burning*
LWT photo

London's Burning has been sold to more than twenty countries worldwide but does not air in the US, as there would be a language problem for most American viewers. Firefighter terms such as "branch," "control," "jet," "shout," and other common daily used words would be unfamiliar to us, as well as some cast members with heavy accents.

American Networks, as well as sponsors, would be envious as *London's Burning*, even after several seasons, still commanded a 45% share of viewers (approximately fourteen million) every Sunday night. However, by season 14, viewers had dropped to 4.8 million.

In 1994, the Lledo Plc toy manufacturer released a series of six diecast models that comprise the *London's Burning* collection to commemorate the history of London's heroic firefighting services. In 1998, Lledo released six additional models with the livery of Blackwall on the doors in the name of the series. Both Lledo sets have "Blackwall Division" under the LFB logo. In January 2000, Richmond Toys Ltd. of Whitton in England released a 1:50 scale Volvo, lettered for the Blackwall station. Many episodes of *London's Burning* are available on video, but only in the European PAL format, so they cannot be viewed on US VCR's. (If you have access to DirecTV, LB can be viewed on the Trio Network on Channel 315 several times weekly).

Three books and two videos (PAL format only) have been produced about the making of the series. British author John Burke penned three novels based on the Blue Watch crew. The London's Burning Club, sponsored by LWT (1994 through 1996), was a fan club that issued newsletters, club packets, and T-shirts, and held competitions and other events in the interests of fire safety. A new website has been established by a different group of the London's Burning Fan Club. Other collectibles available are a board game (1991), and a Fire Kit (1999), which includes a badge (cloth patch), an extinguisher, and other items.

In November 2000, Richmond Toys released a *London's Burning* twenty-piece Emergency Series Playset, featuring a metal and plastic set complete with authentic diecast "Blackwall" London fire engine, Fire station, Helicopters, Support vehicle, Firefighters, Safety barriers, and Road signs. In 2001, an LWT-authorized teapot, replicating the Volvo Engine used in seasons ten through thirteen, down to the license plate was issued. A *London's Burning* Playsuit is currently offered, which includes a helmet with visor, flashlight, firefighter vest, walkie-talkie, fire extinguisher, and axe. A smaller set has a helmet, firefighter vest, and an ID card.

For a unique collectable, technically unauthorized and possibly unintended, is a 'Crane Truck' with the livery of "Blackwall Recovery Unit". In 2000, Golden Wheel Pty., Ltd., of Hong Kong released the 1:87 scale vehicle in their 'Classics Memories' series. Information from the Golden Wheel sales department state, "The logo we use has no special relationship with the TV program (*London's Burning*) and is only what we find in literature". Recovery truck is British terminology for tow truck. The truck is a 1948 Peterbilt, obviously not a British manufacturer. Not a true *London's Burning* collectable but definitely a 'go-with' addition to the collection. The truck also has a Maltese cross on the door with FD NY Company 3 on the shield, which is seen on other fire vehicles of their manufacture. The box depicts a photo of New York's Times Square. There are 10 vehicles in this series, which includes a 1948 Ford fire truck and a tanker with the same door logo and livery of FDNY on its side (not Blackwall). This same casting also comes with the livery of 'Texaco' and 'REA', Railway Express Agency, but called 'Crane with Hoist'.

In Britain, the Fire Brigade typically doesn't respond to medical calls. The ambulance services, whether privately run or volunteer (St John's Ambulance), handle the paramedic duties. For those interested in Paramedic TV programs, since I have mentioned a few already, Britain has a TV program about a hospital and ambulance service, similar to *ER* with Medics. **Casualty** is an hour-long program, which began in 1986 and is still airing, now in its sixteenth season. The drama deals with paramedics and the hospital staff of the fictitious Holby Hospital. It is produced by the BBC, and airs on BBC 1.

Boon was a 1986 drama centering around two middle-aged ex-firefighters, Ken Boon (Michael Elphick), and Harry Crawford (David Daker), who started a business together, after leaving the London Fire Brigade. Boon left the fire brigade after sustaining lung damage when he rushed into a burning building without his breathing apparatus, to rescue a trapped boy in the first episode titled *Box 13*. Crawford retired from the fire brigade to run a bar. The sixty-minute ninety-three episode series ran through 1992, and was produced by Central Independent Television, Plc.

A British version of *Rescue 911*, called ***999***, airs on BBC-1. Often called *Rescue 999*, this fifty-minute reality based program airing on Wednesday evenings, features fire, police, lifeguards, ambulance, and the privately funded air ambulance in dramatic reconstructions of real-life rescues. This long running show began in the spring of 1992. Produced by BBC's Educational division, *999* is hosted by Michael Buerk, who has been with the BBC since 1973. Along with the rescues, the weekly programs cover many first aid topics such as burns, choking, barbecue safety, emergency childbirth, and issues such as escaping from a burning house, a submerged car, and how to avoid being struck by lightning. Some shows feature a "day in the life of" the emergency services, such as spending the day with a watch (shift) at a fire station, London's Helicopter Emergency Medical Service (HEMS), and the Surf Patrol. Rescues from countries around the world including several from the US have also been featured.

999's web site offers "Survival and Safety Guides," "How to become a lifesaver quizzes," and a behind-the-scenes look at the making of *999*. *999* also produce a Lifesaver Video, called "Would you know what to do?" The program spun-off a movie in 1996 titled *999 Lifesavers*. A *Fire Rescue 999* video, narrated by Glenn Murphy, a *London's Burning* actor, containing "real footage of car crashes, blazes, explosions, collapsing buildings, trapped animals, people buried alive, and daring rescues by fearless firefighters" is also available. 999, the UK's equivalent of America's 911 was adopted in England in the 1950's.

"What kind of person is prepared to wade blind through thick smoke, breathe in stomach churning fumes, and dodge leaping flames for a starting salary of about £275 (about $400) a week? Find out in *Firefighters*." These words were taken from a BBC press release about *Firefighters*, a six-part documentary first broadcast on BBC 1 on May 28th, 1997. It was shot between November 1996 and April 1997 on location at Old Swan and Low Hill fire stations in Liverpool, England. It involved a BBC producer, and a camera technician shadowing every single shift of the featured watches over a six-month period. Sometimes, not a single alarm call would come into the fire station; other times, the fire engine and crew would be out firefighting for an entire shift.

The main fire engine at each station was rigged with three digital minicams. One engine, a Dennis Rapier TF202, housed at Old Swan, was involved in a crash during the filming which took it out of service. In addition, one firefighter on each engine had a camera mounted into a specially adapted helmet, and a BBC crewmember with a camera rode on the engine for every single fire call. For the night shifts, some cameras were changed to infrared to enable visibility even in near total darkness.

According to BBC producers, the show was filmed over six months at Merseyside's two busiest fire stations, the series follows the friendly rivalries of two watches: Red Watch at Old Swan, known to their colleagues as "The Adams Family," because of the huge disparity in shape and size of the firefighters, and White Watch at Low Hill, dubbed "The Hollywood Firemen" because of their alleged reluctance to get their hands dirty. Each station deals with over four thousand emergency calls every year, and by using the latest hi-tech remote cameras we got as close to the action as the bravest firefighters themselves." For the BBC, Executive Producer:

Jeremy Mills; Producers: Jennie Cosgrove, Kim Duke; Camera Technicians, Chris Burton, Richard Evans, Dan Lightning.

Reality TV is a satellite channel devoted entirely to all aspects of action-packed, real-life programming. Firefighting, helicopters out-of-control, and sea rescues are some of the incidents captured by cameramen in this hard-hitting series. Documentaries and fly-on-the-wall shows combine with caught-on-camera antics, and hospital-based human-interest stories to bring viewers a wide range of exciting and stimulating television entertainment. *Reality TV* follows the lights and sirens of some of the world's finest rescue squads, chronicling the real lifesaving experiences of paramedics and emergency response units. Police units in hot pursuit, death defying survival stories, real-life events and documentaries; feel the heat as these everyday heroes around the world battle inside burning buildings to save the lives of the trapped and injured.

Reality TV is on air twenty-four hours a day, seven days a week. Zone Vision, UK-based with offices and studios around the globe, is a broadcaster and distributor of international satellite channels and television programs available to cable and satellite viewers in the UK, Europe, South America, Turkey, Israel, the Middle East, and Africa. *Reality TV* is fully localized for its audience via subtitles or dubbed versions of the programs. *Reality TV* is now broadcasting to 3.8 million paying subscribers in ninety-three countries.

FINLAND
Pelastajat (The Rescuers) was a thirty-episode firefighter drama, which aired April 1st through August 17th 1997. Produced by Match-Makers Productions, it aired on FBC (Finish Broadcasting Company) Yle Channel 1, erratically between four and eight times per month. Their website (in Finnish) offers video clips, storyboards, and an episode guide.

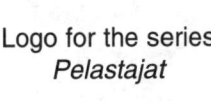
Logo for the series
Pelastajat

A reality-based program titled ***112-Auttajat*** (112-Helping Professionals) featured firefighters, EMS workers, and medical helicopters. The sixteen-part documentary series, based on actual events and situations, began airing July 16, 1999 on TV1. It recounts the day-to-day story of the work of the Helsinki Rescue Services. The series was filmed entirely on location alongside the rescue crews as work around the clock. Produced in Finland by Filmiteollisuus Oy (YLE-1/Filmindustry Limited) in Finland, with Olli Haikka and Jorma Reinilä as producers. 112 is Finland's equivalent of America's 911. In fact 1-1-2 is the single European emergency telephone number for the eighteen-member European Union. Several countries continue to provide their original emergency number (such as 999 in England) for the convenience of the population, as well as 112.

FRANCE

"'To Save or Perish' and 'Courage and Devotion.' Two themes, four strong words, which summarize the ethics of the firemen." These words come from the producer's press release. ***S.O.S 18***, also known as *S.O.S Pompiers* was the title of a ninety-minute drama series that began June 2001, and is now in its second season. It's about the daily lives of professional and volunteer firemen and women, filmed in and around the cities of Mérignac, Bordeaux, and Arcachon, in the Aquitaine region of France. Created and written by Didier Cohen, and produced by Jean-Luc Azoulay, for the France 3 Network, by 2C Associés and Hamster Productions/RTL-tvi/K2/TSR. The series was produced in collaboration with and with the full participation of the Federation of the Firemen of France, with the office of the SDIS (Department of Service of Fire and Safety). *La Vie en Rouge* (Life in Red) was the season's premiere episode. Members of the FNSPF (Federation of the National Sapeurs-Pompiers of France) were on hand to take care that, although the series is fictional in format, it is respectful to the firefighters cause. Technical Advisor is Patrick Péchoux. "18" is the alternate fire department emergency phone number in France.

Cast of *SOS 18*
Photo courtesy of Hamster Productions

GERMANY

Three short-lived programs starting with a production of ***Feuerwache 09*** (Fire Station 9) aired in 1991. This fifty-minute series aired only seven episodes. ***Spritzen-Karli, Der***, (Karl, Squirt That) a forty-five minute series aired only four episodes in 1995. ***Alarm Code 112***, a forty-five minute series aired eleven episodes beginning September 25, 1996. The title song "Fearless Hearts" was sung by England's Chris Norman. (112 is Germany's equivalent of America's 911).

HUNGARY
An animated series, produced by Pannonia Film Studio, titled *Trombi és a Tüzmanó* (Trombi is a Fireman) was aired.

IRELAND
Firewatch was a fast-paced, six-part observational documentary series which first aired in 1999. It followed life in the Phibsboro Fire Station in Dublin, Ireland over a number of months. It captures the real life of the firefighters, as they go about their daily routines of responding to alarms and station duties. *Firewatch* exposes the constant danger, and the intense physical and psychological stress that the team has to endure, such as the delivery of a stillborn child, as well as those calls which amount to nothing more than climbing through someone's back window because they've forgotten their keys. Throughout the series, we see how the firefighters respond to an early morning blaze in a local school, and how they deal with victims who refuse to be helped. One bizarre situation was finding a horse lying in the living room of a person's home that had suffered a heart attack. First airing under the title of *D-Watch*, which is a squad of fifteen firefighters, and five officers. There are three other teams known as A, B, and C watch at the station. *Firewatch* is currently seen on Tara TV, an Irish satellite-based channel seen in Ireland and the UK, on Saturdays at 8.30pm, and on Mondays on RTE One. The documentary was produced by Graph TV Productions, and funded by RTE, the Irish National Public Service Broadcasting Organization.

A new *Firewatch* began airing April 2002 on BBC 1, focusing on several stations of the Northern Ireland Fire Service. The new six-part series, which took a year to film, follows the exploits of firefighters in Belfast, Ballymony, Armagh, and Londonderry. David Kilpatrick produced this series for Straight Forward Productions. "The new series also revealed the incredible sense of comradeship that exists with the service - no matter where a firefighter goes, anywhere in the world they'll be welcomed by their 'brothers,'" says Kilpatrick. An example of this was during filming when the Northern Ireland Fire Service raised $250,000 for their colleagues in New York after the September 11 attacks.

JAPAN
Faiyáman (Fireman), a thirty-minute, sci-fi fantasy adventure series first airing in January 1973. It ran two short seasons with thirteen total episodes. The series starred Naoya Makoto as the fireman, and was directed by Jun Oki for Tsuburaya Productions [jp]. Head writer was Bunkou Wakatsuki.

Kynkyu Hashin Saver Kids (Emergency Rescue Kids) an animated feature series, which ran from February 1991 to February 1992, with an unknown number of original episodes.

MEXICO
Operacion Rescate (Rescue Operations), an hour-long series similar to *Rescue 911.* Airing on Saturdays, host Alexander de Hoyos took viewers into the lives of firefighters, paramedics, the Harbor Patrol, and Coast Guard - men and women who risk their lives on a daily basis. The program accompanied these heroes, and took viewers through the actual emergency call, mobilization of equipment, rescue, and treating of the injured. *Operacion Rescate* did not rely on dramatizations but used authentic footage. Telemax Entertainment produced the series for the Telemundo Network, now owned by NBD, in Tijuana, Mexico.

SINGAPORE
A docudrama titled *Code Red* featured the real-life drama of people caught in a state of crisis, and as a result of urban dangers and stress. Events depicted were fires, people trapped in buildings and vehicles, emergency medical incidents, and situations involving the police. The programs explored the range of human behavior, when people resort to arson, murder, and other crimes, and recreated the drama as it unfolds. In addition to the emergency and police hot-

lines, the program provided information on who to go to for help, such as social agencies, and support groups. Numbers for counseling services and crisis shelters are listed on their web site. *Code Red* was produced by Singapore International Media, and ran through May 1997 with twenty-five episodes. Millie Phuah directed the series.

In association with the National Fire Prevention Council, The Singapore Civil Defense Force (SCDF) sponsors a fire safety docudrama series titled *995*. Presented on the Mediacorp channel, and first telecast in April 2002, this thirty-minute series is presented in English and Mandarin. The series began with prevention of household fires, and will continue with episodes featuring the fire service and emergency ambulance service of the SCDF. Viewers will hear firsthand accounts from fire and burn victims, learn about the effects of burns from specialists, and useful fire safety tips. The Public Affairs department of the SCDF sponsors a contest for "lucky" people to win cash prizes, by answering a few questions shown at the end of the program. *995* is the emergency telephone number of the Singapore Civil Defense Force.

SWEDEN
Nile City 105.6, a five-part miniseries, is an adult comedy set in a fire station that rents out part of their building to a radio station. Produced by SVT Drama [se], the series was filmed on location in Stockholm at the Katarina Fire Station, and first aired January 18, 1995. (The Katarina Station, built in 1876, is a six-bay facility with two engines, one ladder truck, and a fireboat. It is one of ten fire stations protecting a city of two million).

SWITZERLAND
Alarm is a Swiss Reality/documentary TV Show. Airing in 1999 with nine episodes. Reporters accompanied firefighters, along with emergency physicians, and policemen on their difficult and dramatic missions. With some reconstructions, events seen on the

sixty-minute program are police, outpatient clinic, and emergency medicine, the fire brigade, emergency measures, and the safety industry. The viewers received useful tips and information for prevention. The show was presented by Nicole Simmen, and produced by Lava TV in Zurich, Switzerland.

WALES
Fireman Sam is a program created in Wales, Great Britain, in the early 1980's, and still airing on BBC. "A stop-motion cartoon series about the adventures of Fireman Sam, Fire Officer Steele, and Fireman "Elvis" Cridlington, who are ever ready to speed into action on their fire engine called "Jupiter" at the first sign of an emergency, in the town of Pontypandy in Wales." Firefighter Penny was later added to the three-man crew to keep up with the times with female firefighters now in the brigade. Entertaining and subtly educational, this successful series builds a valuable safety message into its episodes. In the UK, Fireman Sam books have sold over five million copies with a further one million video sales. In 1998, ERTL produced a five-inch long die-cast version of "Jupiter." Fireman Sam has spawned products as diverse as playsuits, flashlights, dolls, smoke detectors, and birthday cakes, as well as an award-winning CD-Rom. On the interactive website there are games, stories, fire safety tips, recipes, and more. Production Company - Bumper Films. Co-production partners - S4C/ Heinemann - Reed Books / BBC Video / Prism Art & Design. Narrated by John Alderton.

CHAPTER FIFTEEN — CROSSOVER COLLECTIBLES

Included here are TV shows that, although not fire in format, have produced collectibles that are.

Petticoat Junction, a CBS series airing from 1963 to 1970, featured Uncle Joe (Edgar Buchanan), who lived in the hotel, and was also the Volunteer Fire Chief of Hooterville. The other two members of the department, Smiley Burnette as Captain Charlie Pratt, and Rufe Davis as Secretary Floyd Smoot, were also the engineer and conductor on the Cannon Ball Express. Motel chain Holiday Inn issued a "Member in good standing certificate" from the Hooterville Volunteer Fire Department.

Popular British military comedy series ***Dad's Army*** (1968-1977) set in the fictional south coast seaside town of Walmington-On-Sea during World War II. Of the 80 episodes series seen on BBC, (the last 68 made in color), many are available on video and there was a 1971 cinema version. In one episode, the men of *Dad's Army* sneak into an ammunition dump disguised as firemen. The 'rented' fire engine was manufactured by Leyland, with a registration plate of JL2323 and was built in 1935. It was only seen once in the series. Later, both Lledo (two sets) and Corgi (one set) produced a series of models in the name of the series long after it went off the air. Although given the *Dads Army* tag, the vehicles were not seen in the series They included a 1934 Dennis wheeled escape fire engine by Lledo released in 1991 with the livery of National Fire Service (NFS) and gray color.

The police TV series ***Kojak***, produced by Universal Studios, aired on CBS from 1973 to 1978. In 1977, the Harmony Company produced a plastic set, consisting of a fire chief car, ambulance, stretcher with two EMT's, and a helicopter.

In an episode of the syndicated series ***Baywatch***, the cast was involved in firefighter training, as a result of assisting the FD with a fire on the pier. The lifeguards and the LA County Fire Department form an elite Search and Rescue Unit in the episode titled *Search & Rescue*, which aired in January 1997, and Erik Estrada (*CHiPs*, *Emergency!* 4.12) portrays the Fire Captain. In 1994, Hot Wheels released five-pack emergency vehicle set, which included the "Emergency Rescue" unit in red, using the 1974 casting, with *Baywatch* logos down the side.

Eastenders, a British soap opera produced by the BBC, began airing in 1985, and is still in production. It is the story of a family living in the East End of London, and airs three times weekly in America on PBS stations. In their 1988 "Days Gone" series, the Lledo Plc Toy Company produced five models for The Eastenders Collection, which included a horse-drawn Shand Mason fire engine with the livery of Eastham, London Fire Brigade, Number 17.

Another currently popular British program is ***Heartbeat***, which began airing in 1992. It is primarily a story about a Constable (policeman), and his doctor wife, and is set in the small English town of North Riding in the 1960's. In 1994 the Lledo Plc Company produced several die-cast vehicles in the Heartbeat Collector Series, one of which was a 1950's Dennis Fire Engine, often seen in the program, with the livery of North Riding of Yorkshire. The series is produced by Granada Media Productions for Yorkshire Television.

Goodnight Sweetheart aired in England on BBC 2 from 1993 through 1999 with fifty-seven episodes. It was a romantic comedy set in East London, starring Nicholas Lyndhurst as Gary Sparrow, who lives in the 1990's with his wife, but has a route back in time to war torn England in the 1940's, where he has a mistress. Gary has a tough time keeping his double-life a secret from the two women, as he jumps back and forth in time. Created by Laurence

Marks and Maurice Gran with Alomo Productions and SelecTV, for the BBC (seasons one through three), and the Pearson Television Company (seasons four through six). In their 1996 "Days Gone" series, The Lledo Company produced seven die-cast models in the *Goodnight Sweetheart* series. The 1934 Dennis Fire Engine with the livery of "LCC (London County Council) London Fire Brigade, Whitechapel Division" in dark gray coloring, depicts the type of engine used during WWII, and is featured in *Goodnight Sweetheart* (same casting, different livery used for *Dad's Army*).

Another British program is **Thomas the Tank & Friends**, created in 1945 by Reverend Wilbert Awdry for his ill son, Christopher. Twenty-six books were written about five different steam locomotive trains, before Christopher took over the writing. In 1984, the popular stories were made into an animated TV series, now showing in over one hundred twenty countries, including the US. Among the products made for the program, such as backpacks, videos, and a clothing line, was a Dennis-style fire engine, released in 1999 by Ertl in their Racing Champions series in the name of the program, approximately 2 ¾" in length.

I am sure there are other crossover programs, but I only include a few to show that TV fire collectables can be anywhere.

CHAPTER SIXTEEN — 5 - 5 - 5 - 5

Dating back to the beginning of the fire department, this signal was sent by dispatchers through the old bell system to report that a fireman had died in the line of duty, and that stations were to fly their flags at half-staff. Below are names of people who have died, their achievements and the date of their deaths.

Irwin Allen *Code Red, Towering Inferno*, Producer; honorary Fire Chief in seventy-three cities countrywide, November 2, 1991.

Robert Bray *Lassie* (1964-68), USFS Ranger Stuart Corey March 7, 1983.

Edgar Buchanan *Petticoat Junction*, Uncle Joe, Hooterville Voluntary Fire Chief April 4, 1979.

Smiley Burnette *Petticoat Junction*, Captain Charlie Pratt, Hooterville Voluntary FD February 16, 1967.

Stephen W. Burns *240-Robert*, Deputy Brett Cueva February 22, 1990.

Robert Cinader *Emergency!, Pine Canyon is Burning, The Rangers, Sierra*, Writer, Executive Producer November 16, 1982.

Gary Crosby *905-Wild*, Animal Control Officer, four episodes of *Emergency!* August 24, 1995.

Brad David *Firehouse* (1974), Firefighter Billy Dalzell September 8, 1991.

Jim Davis *Rescue 8*, Rescue Firefighter Wes Cameron April 26, 1981.

Rufe Davis *Petticoat Junction*, Secretary Floyd Smoot, Hooterville Voluntary FD December 13, 1974.

Andrew Duggan *Firehouse* (1973), Capt Jim Parr; *Pine Canyon is Burning,* Capt Ed Wilson May 15, 1998.

Vince Edwards *Firehouse* (1973), firefighter Spike Ryerson March 11, 1996.

Ed Elterman *Rescue 8*, LACo Rescue/firefighter (on real R-8), TA, Retired in 1968. Date of passing unknown.

Lorne Greene *Code Red*, Battalion Chief Joe Rorchek. September 11, 1987.

Dick Hammer *Emergency!* Capt. Hammer, season one - episodes one through ten Oct 18, 1999.

Richard Jaeckel *Firehouse* (1973 & 1974). Firefighter Hank Myers June 14, 1997.

Lang Jefferies *Rescue 8*, Rescue firefighter Skip Johnson February 12, 1987.

Sam Lanier *Emergency!* Dispatcher May 21. 1997.

Julie London *Emergency!* Nurse Dixie McCall October 18, 2000.

Burt Mustin *Leave it to Beaver*, Gus the Fireman January 28, 1977.

Max Phipps *Fire*, Firefighter Edward Martin "Dinosaur" Spence August 6, 2000.

Albert Popwell *905-Wild*, Animal Control Officer April 9, 1999.

James G. Richardson *Sierra, The Rangers,* Paramedic Park Ranger Tim Cassidy; *Emergency!* Paramedic Craig Brice, Writer February 20, 1983.

Nelson Riddle *Emergency!* Theme composer October 6, 1985.

John Smith (Robert "Dutch" Van Orden) *Emergency!* season one - episodes eleven and twelve January 25, 1995.

Morton Stevens *Code Red* Theme composer; *Hawaii Five-0* & seventy-eight other TV themes November 11, 1991.

Bobby Troup *Emergency!* Dr. Joe Early February 7, 1999.

Jack Webb *Emergency!, Sierra, The Rangers, 905-Wild, Pine Canyon is Burning,* Dir., Executive Producer. December 23, 1982.

James Hazeldine, *London's Burning,* firefighter Mike "Bayleaf" Wilson, December 17, 2002.

Virtually the entire cast of *Fire Crackers* has passed on; Alfred **Marks**, The Chief, July 1, 1996; **John Arnet**, Station Officer Blazer, December 21, 1999; **Joe Baker**, Jumbo, May 16, 2001 (also seen in Shelley Long's *Kelly Kelly*, episode 4 in 1998); **Cardew Robinson**, Hairpin, December 27, 1992; **Sydney Bromley**, Whiskers, August 14, 1987; **Ronnie Brody**, Loverboy, May 8, 1991; and the director, **Josephine Douglas**, June 12, 1988.

CHAPTER SEVENTEEN — SPECIAL EFFECTS

A wide variety of special effects are used in motion picture and television production to simulate real events that would otherwise be too dangerous, expensive, or impractical to execute. The types of special effects include fogs, smoke, fire, pyrotechnics, firearms, snow, rain, wind, computer effects, electronics, and miniatures. In the book *Lights! Camera! Safety!,* a Health and Safety Manual for Motion Pictures and Television Production, published in 1991 by Martin McCann Ph.D., some of the hazards in the Arts during the previous fourteen years are discussed. Printed with his permission, excerpts from his book follow:

PYROTECHNICS

"Pyrotechnics special effects are widely used in motion picture production to create all types of effects involving explosions, fires, light, smoke and sound concussions. The types of pyrotechnics materials used include flash powder, flash paper, gun cotton, black powder (gunpowder), smokeless powder, detonator explosives, and many more... The main problems of pyrotechnics include prematurely triggering the pyrotechnic effect, use of larger quantities or more dangerous materials than needed, causing a fire, lack of adequate fire extinguishing capabilities, and, of course, inadequately trained and experienced pyrotechnics operators. As a result of these risks, all pyrotechnics special effects are regulated at the federal, state and local level."

"There shall be at least one trained person on standby fire watch equipped with appropriate firefighting equipment. For major explosions, this could include a full-fledged firefighting crew and truck. The local Fire Department may have specific requirements."

FIRE

"Fire can be used in motion pictures for literally hundreds of scenes. This can include everyday uses of fire such as gas stoves, fireplaces, lit torches, kerosene lamps, bonfires, etc. as well as more destructive fires. The latter can range in scale from burning small items up to burning cars, houses, forests, etc. In many instances these fires are simulated without actually burning the whole structure. A wide variety of flammable and combustible materials have been used to create fire effects, including propane gas burners, rubber cement, gasoline, kerosene, etc. These are often used in combination with pyrotechnics special effects to give the illusion of a fire after an explosion. In stunts involving fire, a specially equipped stunt performer is often coated with a flammable material and set on fire as he or she escapes from a burning building or car."

"Hazards from the use of fire special effects include the involvement of inadequately trained and experienced special effects operators, the fire getting out of control, heat, poor maintenance of fire generating equipment (especially propane equipment), the use of excessive amounts of flammable materials, the presence of combustibles in the area which have not been removed or made fire resistant, and improper storage of combustible and flammable liquids and gases."

"…Over the years, a variety of materials have been developed to make fire effects safer. For example, there are combustible gels and liquid fuels to replace much more hazardous rubber cement, gasoline and other flammable and extremely flammable substances."

"…Any fire special effects should have at least one safety person on standby fire watch equipped with appropriate firefighting equipment. For major fires (e.g. burning of a car or house) this could include a full-fledged firefighting crew and truck."

FOG AND SMOKE

"During the 1980's, the use of fog and smoke to create atmosphere or special lighting effects greatly expanded. However the use of fogs and smokes to create special effects has a history dating back to the early days of film production."

"There are a wide variety of products and machines used to create smoke and fog effects, with varying degrees of hazard. This section only discusses non-explosive materials that depend upon a change in physical state to create the effect, not a chemical reaction... They include dry ice, zinc chloride, ammonium chloride, mineral oil, glycol fogs, and organic burning materials."

"Fog and smoke effects are created by generating a fine mist, a dispersion of very small particles, or an actual smoke by burning organic materials. All smokes and fogs are easily inhaled. Some chemicals used to generate the smoke or fog are toxic; however even chemicals that are not appreciably toxic can be irritating to the lungs. In particular, high risk groups such as people with asthma or other respiratory problems, children, or the elderly."

"Although not as hazardous as pyrotechnics or fire, smoke and fog on motion picture sets is regulated by many Fire Departments. In New York City, for example, you need a fire permit to use smoke or fog, just as you do for pyrotechnics."

CHAPTER EIGHTEEN — INTERESTING TIDBITS

It is said you can gauge how popular a program is by how often it shows up in *TV Guide's* Crossword. Here are some *TV Guide* crossword puzzles with an *Emergency!* tie-in.

June 17, 1972. 42 down, *"Emergency!* star Bobby _____."
                        (Ans: Troup)
October 19, 1974. 39 down, *"Emergency!'s* Roy __Soto."
                        (Ans: De)
December 21, 1974. 14 across, "Randolph Mantooth series."
                        (Ans: *Emergency!*)
March 6, 1976. 1 across, "Fireman Kelly,"
                        (Ans: Chet)
March 6, 1976. 48 across, *"Emergency!* actor."
                        (Ans: Donnelly)
November 11, 1978. 4 across, *"Emergency!* treatment."
                        (Ans: IV)

Not leaving other programs or personalities out in the cold - so to speak:

May 4, 1957. 27 across, "Fire fighting equipment."
                        (Ans: Hoses)
August 24, 1957. 34 across, "TV star, Smokey ___ ___, conservationist."   (Ans: The Bear)
October 31, 1959. 59 across, *"Rescue __."*
                        (Ans: *8)*
February 19, 1972. 3 down, "Smokey _____."
                        (Ans: Bear)
June 15, 1974. 14 across, "Firehouse Bill Overton."
                        (Ans: Cal)

July 17, 1982. 14 down, "*Code Red* star."
(Ans: Lorne Green)
April 7, 1984. 33 across, "Code Red star (initials)."
(Ans: AR (Adam Rich))

From seven different *Summer TV Crossword* puzzles:
29 across, "*Rescue 8* destinations, often."
(Ans: ERS)
4 across, "*Emergency!* nurse Dixie."
(Ans: McCall)
21 down, "Roy Desoto on *Emergency!*"
(Ans: Paramedic)
3 down, "*Emergency!* actor Randolph."
(Ans: Mantooth)
47 across, "*Rescue 8* role."
(Ans: Wes)
25 across, "*Emergency!* emergency."
(Ans: Fire)
40 down, "*Emergency!*'s Dr. Joe."
(Ans: Early)

FIREHOUSES ON TV

Firehouses have been in TV programs that have for the most part absolutely nothing to do with firefighting:

Spenser: for Hire (1985-87), starring Robert Urich, used a vacant (still) 1947 Boston firehouse for his headquarters and residence. It is located at the corner of Mt. Vernon and River Street, in the historic Beacon Hill area of Boston. MTV also used the firehouse in 1997 for their *Real World* TV series.

New York City's home of Ladder 8, at 14 N. Moore St., Manhattan, more recognizable as the *Ghostbusters* Firehouse (exterior shots only), has also been used *The A Team*, *The Pretender*, and an episode of *Seinfeld*.

The series ***Early Edition*** (1996-2000) used an old Chicago firehouse as the stars (Kyle Chandler) place of business, McGinty's Bar.

In an episode of NBC's ***The Pretender***, Jarod (Michael T. Weiss) as Jarod O'Leary in *The Better Part of Valor* uses his genius skills to impersonate a firefighter, while trying to infiltrate a plot involving arson and the death of a firefighter. The final moments of that episode showed Jarod on the apparatus floor of LA City Station 27, the station empty of fire apparatus. There were a couple of exterior shots, and the casual viewer might not have noticed the location since the shot only lasted a few seconds, although anyone who knows the building knew that was the station. They were supposed to be at the house of "The fighting 16th" in Pittsburgh, PA.

During the course of the series, when pretending, Jarod takes on the name of someone associated with his new profession. In other fire-related episodes he calls himself "Jarod Shatner" as a 911 worker,

"Jarod Burns" as an arsonist for hire, and in two different episodes as a forest ranger he took the names of "Jarod Boone" and "Jarod Forrest."

The Profiler - 1996. Used (old) LA City Fire Station 23/Truck 5 as Dr. Sam Waters', (Ally Walker) place of residence in Seasons 1 and 2 with FBI agent's posing as firemen to guard her. All they ever showed was a single shot from the same angle. You never saw Sam entering or leaving, just the exterior of the station. The series local was Atlanta, Georgia.

Buffy the Vampire Slayer also used 23 old LA City Station in one episode of Season 3.

TV SERIES SHOT AT LA CITY FIRE STATION 27

Program	Date Aired	Description
McGyver	October 7, 1991	-*The Pmometheus Syndrome,* Paramount, with Randy Mantooth. Several exterior shots
LA Firefighters	1996	-Fox Network, six episodes
The Pretender	January 11, 1997	-*Better Part of Valor,* NBC, exterior and interior shots, final scenes
Fire Co. 132	1997	-Fox Network, seven episodes (the retitled *LA Firefighters*)
First Response	October 31, 1998	-USA Network, Documentary. Followed a crew of Station 27 for three weeks.
Rescue 77	1999	-WB Network. In one episode at Station 27 - home of a rival group of firefighters.
St. Michael's Crossing	1999	-CBS Network, unaired pilot of fire, police, and EMS drama.

Los Angeles Fire Station 27
Photo courtesy of Los Angeles Fire Department Historical Society

Out of service since 1991 as a result of damage from two major earthquakes, it is now the home of the LA City Fire Museum, which has been completely restored to its former glory, including an elevator. On exhibit at the museum are artifacts and collectibles from several TV programs and movies shot there, and elsewhere throughout the area and around the world.

Built in 1930 for about $100,000, Station 27 initially housed five pieces of apparatus, plus two chief's vehicles, and was the largest station West of the Mississippi with six fire poles. Its three apparatus bays could hold four pieces of equipment each. At the height of activity up to twelve apparatus responded from Station 27. Due to its close proximity to the studios, the motion picture industry frequently made use of the station for filming television and movie scenes calling for fire sequences of apparatus answering alarms. Before *Emergency!*'s Station 51, this was probably the most famous and recognized station.

The new Fire Station 27, which is located at 1327 N. Cole Ave. in Hollywood, just next door to old 27's, has a "Walk of Fame" star in the lobby. It is an official star exactly like the ones found on Hollywood Blvd, and is approved by the Hollywood Chamber of Commerce. Both the "old" and "new" stations have been in countless films, TV shows, commercials, and photo layouts. There is a project in the works to provide stars for two firefighters from Fire Station 27 who have died in the line of duty.

Speaking of "Walk of Fame" stars: Jim Davis (*Rescue 8*), Jack Webb (*Emergency!*), Julie London (*Emergency!*), William Shatner (*Rescue 911*), and Lorne Green (*Code Red*), all have one of the coveted sidewalk stars.

FIRE STATIONS IN THE LOS ANGELES AREA USED IN TV PROGRAMS

Fire Station	TV Program
LA County Station 8 7643 W. Santa Monica Blvd. Los Angeles, CA	*Alarm* - 1954 and 1956. Two unaired pilots. *Rescue 8* - 1958-1960. 73 episodes. *Emergency!* - 1972 pilot-movie *Firehouse* - 1973 unaired preview pilot.
LA County Station 127 2049 E. 223rd St. Carson, CA (just off I-405 at the Arco Refinery)	*Emergency!* 1972-1977, 124 episodes *Emergency!* 1977-1979. Two LA based TV movies.
LA City Station 23 Truck 5 (old) 255 E. 5th St. Los Angeles, CA	*Firehouse* - 1973 - Movie pilot. *The Profiler* - 1996 used as the profiler's home the first two seasons. Exterior location shots.
Beverly Hills Station 2 1100 Coldwater Canyon Dr. Beverly Hills, CA	*Firehouse* - 1974 - series. Thirteen episodes.
LA County Station 110 4433 Admiralty Way Marina Del Rey, CA	*Pine Canyon Is Burning* - 1977 pilot/movie with Kent McCord. *Emergency!* Some episodes

LA City Station 49 400 Yacht St Berth 194 Wilmington (San Pedro), CA	*Code Red* - 1981. Eighteen episodes.
LA City Station 112 444 South Harbor Blvd. Berth 86 Ports O'Call, CA	*The 119* - 1997. Unaired pilot with Kevin Tighe.
Glendale Fire Station 21 (old) 210 S. Orange St. Glendale, CA	*Rescue 77* - 1999. Eight episodes.
LA City Station 46 (old) 1438 W. Vernon Ave. Los Angeles, CA (near the Coliseum)	*Firehouse One* - 1999. Unaired pilot. Fox Television, Sony Pictures *The C-Shift* - unaired. Promos aired in 2002.

It's the Law!

These are actual laws in the states mentioned.

It is against the law in Detroit, Michigan to tie your pet crocodile to a fire hydrant.

In Louisiana, it is illegal to tie an alligator to a fire hydrant.

It is against the law in Marshalltown, Iowa for a horse to eat a fire hydrant.

In Seattle, Washington, no one may set fire to another person's property without prior permission.

In Huntington, West Virginia firemen may not whistle or flirt at any woman passing a firehouse.

In Racine, Wisconsin it is illegal to wake a fireman while he is asleep.

In Danville, Pennsylvania all fire hydrants must be checked one hour before all fires.

The fire department in Charleston, South Carolina may blow up your house to create a firebreak.

The Ft. Madison, Iowa Fire Department is required to practice fire-fighting for 15 minutes before attending a fire.

It is illegal for fire trucks to exceed a speed of 25 miles per hour even when responding to a fire in New Britain, Connecticut.

In Chicago, Illinois it is illegal to eat in a restaurant that is on fire.

In Illinois it is unlawful to change clothes in an automobile with the curtains drawn, except in case of fire.

In Rochester, New York all firemen are required to wear ties.

"FIREMAN" AND "FIRE DEPARTMENT" IN OTHER LANGUAGES

Country	Fireman	Fire Department
Austria	Feuerwehermann	Feuerwehr
Belgium	Brandweeerma	Brandweer
Brazil	Bombiero	Corporacio de Bombeiros
Canada (French)	Pompier	Service 'Dincendie
Czech Republic	Pozarnic	Pozarni Utvar
Denmark	Brandvasenman	Brandvasen
Finland	Palomies	Paloloutios
France	Pompier	Sapeurs Pompiers
Germany	Feuerwehrmann	Feuerwehr
Hungary	Tuzolto	Tuzolto Szervezet
Ireland (Gaelic)	Feartine	Serbhis Toiteain
Italy	Pompiere	Corpo dei Pompieri or Vigili del Fuoco
Luxembourg	Pompjee	Sapeurs Pompers
Mexico	Bombero	Servico de Bomberos
Netherlands	Brandweerman	Brandweer
Norway	Brannmannen	
Panama	Bombero	Cuerpo de Bomberos
Poland	Strazak	Straz Ogniova
Portugal	Bombeiro	Corporacao de Bombeiros
Puerto Rico	Bombero	Servicio de Bomberos
Romania	Pompierilor	
Spain	Bombero	Cuerpo de Bomberos
Sweden	Brandmannens	Brandforsvaret
Switzerland	Fuurehrma	Fuurwehr
Vietnam	Lihn Cuu Hoa	Doi Binhcuu Hoa

EMERGENCY CALL NUMBERS FROM AROUND THE WORLD

The following is just a sampling of the emergency numbers to call to notify fire departments in countries around the globe. The Police and Ambulance services will often have different numbers. The European Union (EU) Countries have adopted a single number, 112, so that anyone traveling within the Union has to remember only one number for all emergency services. That number is indicated as well, along with the original (and still used) number for that country.

	Country number	EU number and Misc.
Australia	000	112 if on cell phone
Austria	122	112
Belgium	100	112
Canada, Ontario	911	
Denmark	112	*
Cape Town, SA	107	
England	999	112
Germany	112	*
Greece	199	
Spain	061	
France	18	112
Finland	112	*
Iceland	112	*
Ireland	999	112
Italy	115	112 Police only
Japan	119	
Liechtenstein	112	*
Luxembourg	113	112
The Netherlands	112	*
New Zealand	111	
Norway	110	112

Pakistan	16	
Portugal	112	115 for forest fires
Finland	112	*
Singapore	995	
Sweden	112	*

* In some cases 112 is the only number available with the former country number discontinued altogether.

CHAPTER NINETEEN — TV PROGRAMS ON THE WEB

To the best of my knowledge, all the links mentioned here are functional and free of objectionable material. However, all areas of these sites have **NOT** been checked. Links are provided for the convenience of the reader. From time to time, URL's change or go offline, and I apologize for any broken links or objectionable material on any of these sites, and any inconvenience this may cause.

If perchance the URL is not functional, search for the program title. For example: *"Burning Flame II"* (with quotes), and then type TV series (try with and without quotes) and hit search. You can even try an actor's name after the title for possibly different results.

Themes for some of the programs below are actual themes, not Midi's.

US TV PROGRAMS

CODE RED
Theme
  http://members.aol.com/Lasta127/CodeRed.wav

EMERGENCY!
  http://www.emergencyfans.com
Theme
http://www.lgoldberg.com/Music/emergcy1.wav   (beginning)
http://members.aol.com/Lasta127/emergncy.wav   (end)
Dispatch tones
http://www.geocities.com/daves_gallery/Sounds/emergncy.wav

MY E! PHOTOS
http://www.emergencyfans.com/gallery/page3/index.htm

FIRE CO. 132
http://www.alexandra-paul.com (click "site map" & then "filmography" and
http://www.alexandra-paul.com/gallery/setof2.jpg

FIREHOUSE (1996)
http://rdanderson.com/film/fire.htm

L. A. FIREFIGHTERS
http://www.geocities.com/TelevisionCity/2822/LAFIRE
Theme
http://www.geocities.com/tvmaniacs/LAFIRE/la-fire.wav

LEAVE IT TO BEAVER
http://www.litb.com/GUS.HTM

PETTICOAT JUNCTION
http://www.dreamwater.net/petticoat/volfiredept.htm

RESCUE 8
Theme
http://www.geocities.com/alcus2/soundrescue.wav

RESCUE 77
http://www.extratv.com/cmp/F99_03_08.htm
Theme
http://www.geocities.com/mr_ballooney/rescue_77.wav

RESCUE 911
http://warhammer.mcc.virginia.edu/cars/resq911.html

TV Firefighters

SMOKEY BEAR
http://www.hotfootteddy.homestead.com/home.html

RESCUE HEROES
http://www.americas-heroes.com

TEST OF COURAGE
http://www.itvs.org/testofcourage/index.html

THE 119 (storyboards)
http://www.famousframes.com/artists/laartists/th/film/119/119.html
http://www.famousframes.com/artists/laartists/th/extra/bws/09.html

THIRD WATCH
http://www.nbc.com/Third_Watch (NBC site)   and
http://www2.warnerbros.com/thirdwatch/home.html (WB site)
       (Season one drawings & photos)
http://www.geocities.com/TimesSquare/Tower/1448/Thirdwatchtext.htm

USAR-1
http://exit3.i-55.com/~gfaller/randy/randy.html

THE BRAVEST
http://www.hearstent.com/HearstSite/Bravest%20folder/bravest1page.html

THE C-SHIFT
http://www.tmg5artists.com/indie.html#THE C-SHIFT

240-ROBERT
http://www.geocities.com/wav240robert/index.html

THE FIRST 24 HOURS
http://www.thefirst24hours.com/

Rescue 911
http://www.cbs.com/primetime/9_11/

SUPERFIRE (56 Photos)
http://www.abcmedianet.com/ph_search/search_lv.htm?prog_num=CB817&text=ffcc00&bgcolor=black

THE FIRESTARTER – JOHN ORR
http://www.courttv.com/onair/shows/mugshots/indepth/orr

INTERNATIONAL TV PROGRAMS

112-AUTTAJAT
http://www.filmiteollisuus.fi/112eng.htm   (English)

999
http://www.bbc.co.uk/health/999/
Theme
http://www.jvsplace.co.uk/tv/999.wav

BURNING FLAME
http://www.geocities.com/TelevisionCity/Network/7781/bfm.htm
            and
http://maggiecheung.5u.com/bf2/bf2-poster.jpg
Theme
http://www.geocities.com/TelevisionCity/Network/7781/bf/bf1.ra

CODE RED (Singapore)
http://www.mediacity.com.sg/codered/index.htm

FIRE
http://australiantelevision.cjb.net
http://coolfreepages.com/fire/fire.html

FIREMAN SAM
http://www.firemansam.co.uk
Theme
http://www.jvsplace.co.uk/tv/Fireman_Sam.wav

FIRE STATION
http://www.lafete.com/firestation

THE FOREST RANGERS
http://www.geocities.com/forestrangers1965/index.html
Theme
http://www.geocities.com/forestrangers1965/forestr2.wav

LONDON'S BURNING
http://www.blackwall-online.co.uk
http://members.lycos.co.ok/blackwallfirestation
http://lonburn.tripod.com
Theme
http://www.the-jps.co.uk/themes/londonsburning.htm
Original
http://website.lineone.net/~the_jps/londonsburning.wav
Current
http://www.btinternet.com/~weavervale/digital/themes/lonburn.mp3

PELASTAJAT
http://www.match-makers.fi/pelastajat/main.html (Finnish)

POLICE RESCUE
http://www.emergencyfans.com/policerescue
http://www.policerescue.com
http://www.police.nsw.gov.au/services/detail.cfm?ObjectID=96&
    SectionID=specialareas

REALITY TV
http://www.zonevision.co.uk/reality/

* Although not TV programs I have included two interesting fire theme web sites: **

BACKDRAFT
http://info2000.net/~rocket/backdraft.htm
http://www.universalstudios.com/unicity/attractions/backdraft.html
Theme
http://www.geocities.com/daves_gallery/Sounds/backdraft.mid
Donald Sutherland (a.k.a. "Ronald" in *Backdraft*) "…Always firemen"
http://www.geocities.com/daves_gallery/Sounds/backdraft.wav

TOWERING INFERNO
http://members.rott.chello.nl/alely

CHAPTER TWENTY — FIREHOUSE RECIPES

As I said in the introduction, not all firefighters are good cooks, although there have been several good firefighter cookbooks published over the years. I have been fortunate to have had two of my recipes published in John Sineno's second book *The New Firefighters Cookbook* published in 1996. Lt. Sineno worked FDNY's Engine 58, and is now retired.

Some departments and even shifts will select their "**cook**" in their own way. Determining the "cook" may be a bit of a trial and error process, with a run of some indescribable and infamous dishes prepared, both good and bad. Some may rotate the cooking responsibilities amongst the station personnel, to vary the types of dishes prepared. Some firefighters have even taken cooking classes, and once that is discovered they usually become the '**designated cook**.'

The gathering of food for the day will most definitely depend on the specific department. Some chiefs forbid the use of Engine Companies, Trucks, Squads, etc., to go to the store on duty, so the food must be purchased by the "cook" on his or her day off. In other departments, the visual of the firefighters in the store shopping is considered good public relations. Often firefighters are stopped by individuals and thanked for services rendered to them or a family member during an emergency. In many cases, we have no clue what incident they are talking about, as often it's the other shift that deserves the credit. And yes, we do park in the RED zone; after all we are riding a red emergency vehicle.

The recipes that follow are either my own, or from other firefighters that I have traded with over the years. They have graciously allowed me to include them here and are so acknowledged.

Terminology, although seemingly obvious, I will go over. This too will vary slightly from department to department. Engineer Joe Henson of the LA County Fire Department has provided the following. (I used to work with his ex-wife, and she admits she can't boil water, so it's a good thing someone was able to cook in the family).

Most stations will have a bell or intercom system for the cook to announce "**chow**." Back in the dark ages before intercoms, a hanging bell or cooks triangle was rung. The bell has probably been in the station for years, or if it's a new station someone may donate a bell, which the firefighters will hang up.

In large stations that have several personnel on duty, there is usually an assistant cook called the "**bull cook**." The bull cook is either a scheduled bull cook or someone who volunteers to help the "**cook**."

The scheduled cook compiles a grocery list, and the engine company, or whatever fire apparatus the cook is on, will go to the store (if permitted). That morning all personnel pitch in the amount of money needed, or sometimes it's a set amount. You're either **"in or you're out,"** as far as the meal is concerned. Sometimes, personal preference will dictate whether an individual will eat the cook's evening meal or not. For the most part, whether we eat the prepared meal, or something we prepared ourselves, we usually all eat together, as this is probably the only time we get a chance to sit down and be together. In a house with only three or four firefighters, it's not as difficult, but in a large house with multiple pieces of equipment, and seemingly one of them always out on a call of some sort, it is tough to get everyone together at one time.

In many stations, the person "**in the tank**" is the one doing the dishes, which may be decided by various games of chance, or simply rotated among the firefighters. In most stations, the "cook" is never in the tank, as he prepared the food. If the cook must participate, he gets an automatic win (as it usually takes two wins to **"get out."** Once you're **"out"** it comes down to the last two players, as they play off to determine who will be **"in the tank."** The runner-up will usually be saddled with the light-duty work, such as sweeping, emptying the trash, and finally mopping the floor. The person **"in the tank"** empties the dishwasher, and makes sure everything is cleaned and put away. Before dishwashers, all dishes and anything else used to prepare the meal was hand washed, hand dried, and put away. Air-drying was not allowed.

Preparing Thanksgiving dinner for families and the firefighters.
L-R: Carl McAllister, Author Richard Yokley, and Tim Isbell

CAPTAIN'S CHICKEN

Ingredients: (may vary a bit – I've never made it the same way twice)
4 lbs Chicken (whole or breast pieces)
1 large onion, chopped
1-2 cloves garlic, chopped
1 large bell pepper, chopped
1 large can diced stewed tomatoes
1 can tomato soup
½ to 1-cup salsa (mild or hot to taste)
1 can green chilies, sliced
1 tsp parsley
¼ tsp pepper
2 tbs Worcestershire sauce
½ cup mushrooms, sliced
Minute rice or steamed rice
Directions:
If using whole chicken – Boil to remove bones. If using pieces – boil or pan fry until no longer pink. Set aside in large pot. Sauté onion, garlic, and bell pepper, and add to chicken. Add tomatoes, soup, salsa, and seasonings. Bring all to the boil, and simmer for <u>at least</u> an hour. Add green chilies and mushrooms fifteen minutes prior to serving. Serve over rice. Serves four to six. Add more of everything if larger firehouse.

TACO SOPEAR (DIP)

Ingredients:
1 large can refried beans
1 jar salsa (or fresh made) medium to hot (depending on taste)
1 can chopped olives, drained
1 4 oz can diced, peeled, green chilies
2 large avocados, peeled, pitted, and mashed
1 16 oz container sour cream
Hot carrot slices
Onion rings
Jalapeno peppers
Grated cheddar cheese
Tortilla chips

Mix refried beans with half the salsa. Spread mixture over bottom of serving bowl. Layer with olives, green chilies, salsa, avocados, and sour cream. Garnish dip with hot carrots, each within center of onion ring and jalapenos. Sprinkle with cheese.

OUT-OF-SEASON LOBSTER

Ingredients:
2 lbs white fish fillets
2 bay leaves
1 onion, sliced
lemon slices
½ to ¾ cup dry vermouth
Melted butter
Parsley and lemon wedges for garnish

Place fish in deep saucepan. Cover with water. Add bay leaves, onion, lemon slices, and vermouth. Bring to the boil, reduce, and simmer for eight to ten minutes (or until fish starts to break apart). Remove from pan. Serve with melted butter and garnish. Tastes just like lobster (well, almost).

The last two recipes were published in *The New Firefighters Cookbook* (1996) by Lt. John Sineno, FDNY Engine 58 in Harlem, the Fire Factory, to benefit the NY firefighters Burn Foundation.

SPAGHETTI
(Serves at least 100 people)

Sauce Ingredients:
3 lb sausage
5 to 7 lbs hamburger
3 No. 10 cans tomato purée
2 No. 10 cans peeled, whole tomatoes
¾ cup sugar
2 large bell peppers, chopped
4 large onions, chopped
½ cup garlic powder
2 tbs salt
¾ cup Italian seasoning
1-cup parsley
4 cups sliced mushrooms

Directions:
Brown sausage and hamburger. In a large pot add the mixture- tomato puree, crushed peeled tomatoes, sugar, and salt. Mix and bring to the boil. Add onions and bell pepper. Reduce and simmer for <u>at least</u> an hour. Add garlic and Italian seasoning. Simmer for three to six hours (at least). Stir occasionally, careful not to scrape the bottom of the pan too hard. Thin with water as needed or desired. ½ hour before serving add parsley and mushrooms.

Place the saucepot in another pan with three to four inches of water on the stove. Use a grill or other device to keep pot from directly touching the pan. This stops the mixture from burning on the bottom. Do not let the water dry out.

Sauce will taste much better if prepared the day before so ingredients will have a chance to blend.

Cooking times are a minimum. Simmer over night if possible. Might have to have the probie stand fire watch.

Spaghetti: Cook 10 lbs of noodles (will be much easier if prepared the day before serving - less stress). Cook noodles and place in large pans with ice, cover with plastic wrap, and place in refrigerator. On the day of serving, remove from refrigerator as needed, place in boiling water for only about two minutes to refresh.

Salad:
10 heads lettuce
200 cherry tomatoes
Oil/vinegar dressing
Croutons
**Don't forget the Garlic Bread

GARLIC, CHEDDAR CHEESE, AND CHIPOTLE MASHED POTATOES

36 garlic cloves
8 oz grated, sharp (or extra sharp) cheddar cheese
4 oz cream cheese (room temp)
½ stick (1/4 cup) unsalted butter or margarine
1/3 cup olive oil

1½ tsp minced canned chipotle chilies
5 lbs russet potatoes, peeled, cut into 1 inch pieces

Preheat oven to 350 degrees F.
Toss garlic with oil in baking pan, cover with foil, and bake for thirty minutes. Uncover and bake for fifteen minutes. Cool, peel, and chop. Cook potatoes in large pot of boiling, salted water until tender (about twenty-five minutes). Drain and transfer to large bowl. Add garlic and remaining ingredients. Beat mixture until smooth. Serves eight to ten.

Can be prepared two hours ahead. Simply cover and let stand at room temperature.
Reheat when needed, stirring occasionally, then serve.

GARLIC, CHEDDAR CHEESE, AND CHIPOTLE MASHED POTATOES
"Lo-fat version"

Using most of the same ingredients: substitute low-fat whipped cream cheese for cream cheese; eliminate butter and use liquid from potatoes with Swanson chicken broth. Take potatoes, dollop of cream cheese, cheddar cheese, chili, garlic, potato broth, and Chicken broth, and blend a little at a time. You can take a whole garlic head, cut a small portion off the top, and roast in a foil package with a little oil. When cooked, squeeze cloves out and add to mixture while blending to your liking. Bake at 350F.

Variation: Onion mashed potatoes: Slice several yellow onions (Vidalia, Walawala, or Maui works well!). Caramelize the onions and then add to the milled potatoes at the end.

BEWARE OF THE HABANERO CHILIES...

On July 23rd 2001, it wasn't firehouse chili that sent four San Diego lifeguards to the hospital. "This was 3rd Alarm Lifeguard Chili," quipped lifeguard Lt. Rick Wurts. "Noxious fumes prompted the evacuation of lifeguard headquarters, and a three-story tower at 6:30pm for half an hour today. Four of the five lifeguards on dispatch duty had trouble breathing, and felt sick from the fumes. The four were taken to the hospital, examined, and released. We evacuated the whole building, donned our breathing apparatus, and then went back in to check the tower, to determine the source of the noxious fumes. The best we could find out, it was the Habaneros chilies roasting in the oven. We took them out and the air cleared," Wurts said.

Wurts said a lifeguard had put the extra-hot peppers into the oven to roast. The peppers did not catch fire but the heat released chemicals into the air that made some people ill.
(Pauline Repard - San Diego Union-Tribune)

MARCO LOPEZ FROM *Emergency!* WITH HIS FAMOUS CHILI RECIPE
(printed with permission from his cookbook)

1 large onion coarsely chopped
1 medium green pepper chopped
1 large celery stalk chopped
1 large clove garlic minced
3 tablespoons oil
4 pounds ground beef chuck
1 1/2 teaspoons minced jalapeno chili
1/2 cup chili powder
1 tablespoon ground cumin
1 teaspoon garlic salt
1 teaspoon onion salt
1 teaspoon liquid red pepper seasoning
2 bay leaves crumbled
2 teaspoons salt
1/4 teaspoon freshly ground black pepper
2/3 cup beer
1 (16ounce) can stewed tomatoes
1 (8ounce) can tomato sauce
1 (6ounce) can tomato paste
2 tablespoons honey
1 1/2 cups water (about)

Stir fry onion, green pepper, celery and garlic in oil in large dutch oven, pan or kettle for 8 minutes or until tender and golden brown. Add beef and cook until crumbly. Add jalapeno chili, chili powder, cumin, garlic, salt, onion salt, red pepper, seasoning, bay leaves, salt, pepper, beer, tomatoes, tomato sauce and paste, honey, and enough water to barely cover ingredients. Cook over low heat, uncovered, stirring often, for at least 3 hours or until chili is thick and flavors are well blended. Adjust seasoning to taste if necessary (10-12 servings).

Marco's cookbook of over thirty recipes (and still growing), which he prepared for the cast and crew of *Dragnet* and *Emergency!* is available for purchase. Contact Rozane, who handles Marco's orders, at rozane@emergencyfans.com. The book also includes some photos of him on the *Emergency!* set.

"The *Emergency!* cast also had fun by throwing the best parties around," Lopez said. "There were about fifteen other television series getting made at the same location, and everybody used to invade our parties." Lopez also used to enjoy cooking for the company in the set kitchen. This was the biggest similarity between the real Lopez, who has been to culinary school, and his character.

Firefighter cooks I know have provided the following recipes. They have graciously allowed me to share with you some of their favorites.

GRILLED FISH

Ingredients:
For marinade, combine:
2 tbs melted butter
¼ cup Italian Dressing
1 garlic clove, diced thin
Pinch of black pepper
Juice from ½ lemon
Directions:
Place fish fillets in marinade for twenty minutes. Wrap in aluminum foil for grilling. Grill three to four minutes each side over high heat. Remove and Voíla... enjoy!

VEGETABLE MEDLEY

Ingredients:
Two whole carrots, peeled and chopped
½ to whole broccoli, chopped
¼ onion, sliced
1 bell pepper, sliced

Preheat wok for ten minutes on high heat. Add ingredients. Reduce heat to medium, and add three teaspoons olive oil. Cook for twenty minutes, and serve with fish over a bed of steamed white rice.

These recipes come from Tony Davis, Highland California Fire Department Station 541.

BRITISH FARE

Cheese Sandwiches

I am not sure of the origins of the meal, but it is eaten at the morning break at around 10:30am. It is known as "stand easy," the traditional Royal Navy term for a tea break. Cheese sandwiches were traditionally prepared by the mess manager (while the cook was preparing lunch). The sandwiches, normally two per person, are made from a large white loaf of crusty bread, cut into thick slices about ¾" thick (known as "door stops"), and filled with grated Cheddar cheese.

The "stand easy" is traditionally served with sliced raw onions. Some watches do serve rolls (buns), or baps (a large, soft floured bread roll, normally cut in two). The names for bread rolls vary depending on where you are in the UK, and north of England it's called a "cob." Tomatoes and other salad appeared much later. Some watches combined "stand easy" and lunch, with a late breakfast at 11:00am, consisting of fried eggs, bacon, sausage, black pudding, fried bread, tomatoes, baked beans, and toast. This is known as a "fat boys breakfast" or just "fat boys."

I can only assume that the cheese sandwiches became traditional because they were simple and quick to prepare, and were made from easily obtained ingredients. Watches at some stations became famous for their "stand easy" with a spread fit for royalty. At Lambeth (headquarters station) we had traditional "stand easy" and at Brixton we had a "fat boys."

Pete Gwilliam, London Fire Brigade

The fireboat 'Phoenix', also based at Lambeth station on the river Thames, ate their meals on the boat and not in the station mess. If the weather was bad they ate ashore, if good then a picnic on the Thames was in order!

Author having cheese sandwiches with the crew of London Fireboat Phoenix while on holiday.

TV Firefighters

For US firefighters it's **Five Alarm Pasta**, and for us UK firefighters it's **Arson Fire Pasta**. It makes a good, quick, tasty meal for busy occasions when shouts (alarms) are coming in fast and furious, and you don't have a great deal of preparation time.

Ingredients:
1kg (2 ½ lbs) pasta
3 cans chili 'cook-in sauce'
2 cans chopped tomatoes
Small jar of pesto sauce
Chili sauce, salt and pepper to taste, and grated cheese
Directions:
Cook pasta and drain. Place in ovenproof dish. Pour in 'cook-in sauce,' chopped tomatoes, pesto sauce, chili sauce, salt, and pepper. Place in oven 180c (350 F) for twenty minutes. (Place two toilet paper rolls in freezer). Remove pasta from oven, cover with grated cheese, and zap under the grill to melt the cheese.

Serve with tortilla chips and a large jug of ice water or a cold jug of Bud! Note: I'm not sure what the cans of chili cook-in sauce mix is called in the States, but in the UK it is a ready made mixture of chili beans in a chili sauce with minced lamb already in it.

Serves six
Cold toilet paper as needed!

Pete Gwilliam, London Fire Brigade, Retired
Author: 'Cook-in sauce' comes in a variety of flavors such as, sweet and sour, curry, Mexican, and with chili, in a can or pouch. My last visit to England confirmed that 'cook-in sauce' as used in this recipe is cans of chili con carne. Chili sauce used is packets of chili seasoning, such as McCormick or Lawry's.

Unfortunately I was unable to locate "Arse on Fire" Hot Sauce (hence the recipe name), which I am told is quite hot.

TOAD IN THE HOLE

Toad in the Hole is a Traditional English recipe originating from Yorkshire, a county in the north of England.
Ingredients:
100g (4oz) plain flour
1/2 level tsp salt
1 egg
270ml (9fl.oz) milk
225g (8oz) pork sausages (Other herby sausages can be used, including vegetarian ones).

Directions:

1. Preheat the oven to 200C (400F), and grease a shallow ovenproof dish or Yorkshire pudding tin (or a large fairly shallow dish, such as a lasagna pan).
2. Place the flour, egg, milk, and salt in a large mixing bowl, and whisk until smooth and lump free.
3. Place the sausages in the greased dish in a single layer, then pour over the batter. Bake in the oven for forty to forty-five minutes until well risen and golden. Try not to open the oven door during cooking or the pudding may not rise. Serve immediately with onion gravy, and chopped cabbage, or other green vegetable. Serves 4.

TOAD IN THE HOLE
ALTERNATIVE RECIPE

Ingredients:
25 g (1 oz) butter
450 g (1 lb) sausages
110 g (4 oz) flour
1 egg
300 ml. (10 oz) milk
Directions:
1. Pre-heat oven to 220C (425F)

2. Place butter and sausages in a 25x30 cm (10 x 12 inch) roasting tin. Cook for ten minutes (or longer if you like your bangers very well done).

3. Sift the flour into a bowl. Break in the egg. Gradually add half the milk, beating to form a smooth batter. Pour in the remaining milk, and beat until quite smooth. Alternatively, add the flour, milk, and egg in a blender, and blend until smooth.
4. Pour the batter into the roasting tin and bake for forty to forty-five minutes, or until the batter is well risen and golden.

If in a real hurry you can substitute hot dogs and pancake mix for the batter...kids love it!

HEARTY BEEF & POTATO CASSEROLE

4 cups frozen tater tots
1 medium tomato, chopped
1 pound ground beef
1 can cream of celery soup
1 (10 oz) package frozen chopped broccoli, thawed
1/3 cup milk
1 (2.8 oz) can Durkee French fried onions
1 cup (4 oz) shredded cheddar cheese
1/4 tsp garlic powder
1/8 tsp black pepper

Place potatoes on bottom and upsides of 8x12 inch casserole. Bake uncovered at 400 degrees for ten minutes. Brown beef in large chunks, and drain. Place beef, broccoli, ½ can onions, and tomato in potato shell. Combine undiluted soup, milk, half-cup cheese, and seasonings. Pour over beef mixture. Bake covered at 400 degrees for twenty minutes. Top with remaining cheese and onions. Bake covered for two or three minutes longer. Serves 6.

GLORIFIED BAKED BEANS

2 (16 oz) cans baked beans
1 lb ground beef, browned
1 pound bacon, fried crisp and crumbled
1-cup brown sugar
1/2-cup sugar
1-cup catsup
1 cup barbeque sauce

Mix all ingredients together in a 9x13 inch pan. Bake at 350 degrees for forty-five minutes.

CREAM CHEESE BROWNIES

1 large box brownie mix
1 (8 oz) package cream cheese
1/3-cup sugar
1/2 tsp vanilla
1 egg

Prepare brownie mix. Spread half the mixture into a 9x13 inch pan. Beat softened cream cheese, sugar, vanilla, and egg. Spread cream cheese mixture over brownie mix. Spoon remainder of brownie mix on top. Swirl with a knife. Bake at 350 degrees for 35-40 minutes.

[Capt. Scott Miller, Compton FD CA, retired].

FIREHOUSE CHILI

Ingredients:
3 cans kidney beans
2 cans chili beans
3 lbs ground beef
1 onion, diced
1 container sliced mushrooms
3 large cans crushed tomatoes
Chili powder

Brown ground beef, and throw in diced onion and mushrooms. Mix in large pot... beef, beans, and tomatoes. Bring to the boil and reduce heat. Add chili powder to taste, and let simmer for two hours. Serve in Sourdough baguettes or with corn bread. Serves 6.

TUNA CASSEROLE

2 large cans tuna, in water
1 bag egg noodles
1 onion diced
1 small can mushrooms
2 large cans cream of mushroom soup
1 small can peas
Sharp cheddar cheese
French fried onions
Boiled noodles
Mix drained tuna, noodles, soup, onion, peas, and mushrooms in large bowl. Scoop into casserole dish. Top with shredded cheddar and French fried onions. Bake at 350 for an hour. Let cool for five to ten minutes. Serve with veggies. Serves 4-6.

CHICKEN FAJITA BURRITOS

1 lb chicken breast, skinless, boneless
1 red bell pepper, sliced
1 yellow bell pepper, sliced
1 purple onion, sliced
1 packet fajita mix
1 large can refried beans
Flour tortillas
Salsa

BBQ chicken and slice into strips. Sauté onion and bell peppers in olive oil until just tender. Add chicken and fajita mix. Keep on low heat, adding water if needed. Warm beans and tortillas, spread some beans onto tortilla, and then add fajitas. Wrap into burrito.

Enjoy. Engineer Carl McAllister, Bonita-Sunnyside Fire Department (Previous 3 recipes).

FIREHOUSE MEATS COOKED TO PERFECTION

By following the simple guidelines below you can become a hit in any firehouse, anywhere in the world, and learn how to serve firehouse meats cooked to perfection.

Many successful firehouse cooks have learned how to cook meat so it is flavorful, tender, and doesn't require a lot of monitoring. Oh yeah, and it has to be as inexpensive as possible.

Select the meat of your choice, find the grocery store that determines what meat will be the best that day and they do so by placing that cut on sale. Firefighters are also known for bringing in a wide variety of game (usually dead) to the firehouse, with things like boar, elk, moose, bear, and venison to name a few. This recipe is really just guidelines and can be used for just about anything accept for fish.

To start the cooking process, select a large frying pan or a Dutch oven, something that can go into the oven and has a lid. Most firehouses have cast iron pots and pans that have been around for long periods of time (decades). They are good to cook in, save the taxpayers money (replacement cost), and are one of the few things that we don't break very often.

If you have selected a cut that is thinly cut (approx. 1/4" to 1" thick) you will want to serve this kind of meat in gravy. This style of cooking keeps the thin meat moist so that if you get that long run in the middle of cooking you can change the main menu item from meat to soup. Other items to get at the store include 4-5 medium onions, garlic cloves, and your favorite seasonings. Some of the good fire chefs use Lawry's Seasoning Salt, but the great ones make it happen at the station spice rack. (It's a great one's trade secret of what to use in the spice rack . . .)

Rinse and pat the meat dry, cut meat into desired serving portions, season the meat to taste (both sides), dust the meat with seasoned flour (shake in a paper bag with the flour seasoned with the same or similar seasoning as you put on the meat), and quick fry the meat in cooking oil. During the quick frying process you are looking for a light golden color. The meat will still be raw inside, but that's okay because it will finish cooking in the baking process.

After you have quick fried all of the meat pieces, set it aside while you prepare the gravy. Pour off most of the frying oil until you have enough to cover the bottom of the pan/pot. (Save the extra oil just in case you need a little more). In the same pot or frying pan the meat was cooked in, leave enough oil to cover the bottom on the pan. When the oil is warm add all 4 of the rough chopped onions. Cook the onions over medium heat until brown. Next add minced garlic to taste, 2 to 3 cloves, and cook until soft.

Now if you can still see some oil in the pan, through the onions, garlic and seasoning then add 1 cup of all-purpose flour to the frying oil. If you can't see some oil add some of the reserved oil prior to adding the flour. This is the point where the great one's rise to stardom because they know that all of the flavor is now being combined with the flour. Over medium to low heat use a fork to stir the flour until it is light to medium brown. This process is called a "rue " in French and Cajun cooking. When your rue is a nice color, add enough cold/cool water to make soupy gravy. A whisk will help you get out any lumps. Now turn up the heat to med/high and return the meat to the pot. The gravy will thicken as the pot comes to a boil. Once the gravy reaches a medium boil check the taste and adjust the seasoning. When it tastes kind of right, place the cover on the pot and remove from the stovetop. Place the covered pot into a preheated oven set at 250° and walk away. One to two hours later check the meat for tenderness with a fork and make any final adjustments to the seasoning. Serve with rice or potatoes, veggies and rolls.

If you chose a piece of meat that is 1 ½ " thick up to the big roast size then the cooking process is much easier.

Rinse and dry the meat, season with your favorite seasonings, (the great ones will now pierce the meat and push cloves of garlic into the holes). In a hot pot/pan add enough oil to cover the bottom, quickly sear the meat on all sides until each side has a light brown crust. Remove meat from pan. Next add the rough chopped onions and garlic to taste into the pan. Place the meat on top of the onions. Add approx. ½ cup of water or your favorite wine into the pot. Cover and place into a 500° oven for ½ hour.

After ½ hour reduce the oven temperature to 250° and cook for 3 to 4 hours. Check meat for tenderness every hour of cook time by placing a fork into the meat. When the fork is easily twisted in the meat it is done and ready to serve. If it is not tender, increase the temperature to 300° for the next hour of cooking. When the meat is done remove it from the pan and let it rest for 10 minutes. While the meat rest, return the pot to the stovetop and bring the juices to a med boil. Add ¼ cup of cornstarch into a tall glass, pour ½ cup of cold water over the cornstarch and stir with a fork until there are no lumps. Pour cornstarch mixture into the boiling pot on the stove and stir with a whisk until gravy is smooth. Readjust seasoning to taste and serve with rice or potatoes.

Russell Steppe, Engineer, San Diego Fire Department
(Author: Russell IS one of the 'great ones' when it comes to firehouse cooking.)

ACKNOWLEDGMENTS

A special thanks to the many people whom I have literally "bugged" over the years for their valuable assistance in the research of this book, with an untold number of questions. All of who gladly (I think) shared their time, experience, and patience. Please forgive me if I have missed anyone. They are as follows:

* **Mary Cleary**, Susan Johnson in *Rescue 8*
* **Jim Perry**, Captain II, LAFD Retired, Technical Advisor, *Firehouse*, series, 1974
* **James O. Page**, Battalion Chief, LACoFD, Retired, Technical Consultant, writer, *Emergency!*
* **Marco López**, actor, cook, *Emergency!*
* **Dick Baker**, Battalion Chief, LAFD, Retired, Technical Advisor, *Code Red*,   pilot episode
* **Blair Lamere**, LA City Paramedic, Retired, Snyder Ambulance Company
* **Holly Morris** & **Penny McGuire**, LWT, *London's Burning* (UK)
* **Peter Gwilliam**, Station Officer London Fire Brigade, Retired. Extra, featured in *999*, and the movie and episodes of *London's Burning*.
* **Wanita Smit**, *Fire*, (Australia)
* **Tony Cavanaugh**, Creator, Writer, and Producer of *Fire* (Australia)
* **Tom Lupo**, Director & Co-Executive Producer, *Firefighters* (1993)
* **Wendy Leonard**, Head writer, *Firefighters* (1993)
* **David Daugherty**, Paramedic, Haz Mat, LACoFD, Technical Advisor, *Rescue 77*
* **Laura Lambert**, Asst. Set Decorator, *Third Watch*
* **Joanna Giddon**, Sr. Press Manager – NBC Entertainment
* **John Lavet**, NBC Photo department

* **James P. "Turk" Raftery**, FDNY Dispatcher, Manhattan/Citywide operations
* **Marc Doré**, Firefighter Engine 54, FDNY
* **Joe Ciscone**, Firefighter Grade A, East Haven CT
* **Keith "Nick" Nicoliello**, fireman FDNY, Ladder 30, extra and chauffer on *H.E.L.P.*
* **Mark Stone**, Captain FDNY, EMS Medical Supervisor Battalion 8, Manhattan
* **Tim Brown**, FDNY Rescue 3 & OEM, Technical Advisor, *Firehouse* (1996)
* **Joe Brosi**, Lt. FDNY Fire Marshall Extra - *Firehouse* (1996)
* **Paul Schneider**, Curator, LACoFD Fire Museum
* **Greg C. Jensen Sr.**, The Efx Shop, special effects for *The 119*
* **Jim Featherstone**, Captain LAFD, Technical Advisor, *The 119*
* **Brian Humphrey**, Firefighter/Specialist, Paramedic, LAFD Public Service Officer.
* **Scott B.Miller**, Captain, LACoFD, Retired. Extra, set medic, and Technical Assistant in Movies & TV programs
* **Ted Farmer**, Captain, Yosemite Concessions Service, Yosemite National Park
* **Raul Moreno**, Production Manager at CBS Television
* **Dr. Michael McMann**, author
* **Sammy Fox**, firefighter/paramedic, San Luis Obispo FD
* **Leena Mäenpää-Bentley**, Production Manager, Filmiteollisuus TV-1, *112-Auttajat*
* **Louise Lehoux**, Sovimage Production Company (Quebec), *Caserne 24*
* **Lee Goldberg**, author, TV writer, and producer
* **Chin Thammasaengsri**, Writer & Executive Producer, *The C-Shift, Engine Company X*
* **Russell Steppe**, Engineer, SDFD, Producer, *The Men of Station 19*
* **Jean Curley**, video archivist & researcher
* **Dan Forrer**, Executive Producer, *In The Line of Duty*
* **Steve Cole**, Director of Factual Programming, *REALITY TV*

TV Firefighters 253

* **Trish Hayes**, BBC, Archives researcher
* **Wendy Earle**, bfi (British Film Institute), Resource Editor
* **Winnie Ho**, Manager, and **Janet Wan**, Asst. Manager Corporate and Community Relations, External Affairs Division, Television Broadcasts Limited (TVB) Hong Kong, *Burning Flame & Burning Flame II*
* **Deirdre Gunning**, Media Communications Executive, Tara TV, Ireland
* **Sue Bennett**, ABC (Australian Broadcasting Co.), Asia-Pacific Network
* **Mark Jeanette**, Bay News Video
* **Mike Lewis**, LACoFD, Paramedic/Engineer, Retired. TA, *Emergency!*
* **Jay Johnson**, Emergency-One Inc., Vice-President of Marketing, Ocala, Florida
* **Don Croucher**, Crown Firecoach Enthusiasts, SPAAMFAA Historian
* **Andy Holzli**, Superior Emergency Vehicles Ltd., (Superior E-One) of Alberta, Canada
* **Cinema Vehicle Services**, Ray Claridge, President
* **Fire Protection Specialists** (Frandango Inc.)
* **Cindy Fralick**, Captain, LACoFD, *Firefighters*, TVMovie of the week
* **Luke Williams**, Ocean Lifeguard Specialist, Lifeguard Community Services, County of Los Angeles Fire Department
* **Brent Burton**, firefighter LACoFD. Extra *Firehouse One, Engine Co. X*
* **Barry Walter**, Queensland Msr. Specialized Vehicles, Austrailia
* and **Erika and Rozane's** *Emergency!* website

As you can see, during the seven years that it has taken to research the subject of TV FIREFIGHTERS many people including writers, producers, actors, etc., were contacted for their information and input, more than you see listed here. I used e-mail, the postal service, and the phone. Unfortunately, some chose not to respond or assist, even after repeated attempts, or I simply could not get through the myriad of people to get to the person with the requested information. I have put together what I have with the information at hand. I have tried to confirm and reconfirm sources and information, before inclusion. In some cases, unfortunately, this was not always possible.

BIBLIOGRAPHY

TV Time '74, 1974 by Peggy Hertz, Scholastic Book Services, N.Y.

TV's Top Ten Shows, and their stars, 1976, by Peggy Hertz, Scholastic Book Services, N.Y.

TV Book, The Ultimate Television Book, 1977, edited by Judy Fireman, Workman Publishing Co.

TV Album, 1978, by Peggy Hertz, Scholastic Book Services, N.Y.

The Paramedics, 1979, by James O. Page, Backdraft Publications, New Jersey

TV80, 1979, by Lisa Freeman, Scholastic Book Services N.Y.

The Great TV Sitcom, 1983, by Rick Mitz, Perigee Books – Putnam Publishing Group, NY

Movies Made for TV - 1964-1984, 1984, by Alvin H. Marill, New York Baseline Books, Pub.

The Firehouse, An Architectural and Social History, by Rebecca Zurier, 1982 Abbeville Press, Inc.

The Complete Encyclopedia of Television, Vol. 1: Series-Plots-Specials, 1937-1973 by Vincent Terrace 45th Edition, July 1985, Baseline Books, Pub

Los Angeles Fire Department: A Century of Service, 1986, by Paul Ditzel, Fire Buff House – New Albany Indiana and Los Angeles (City) Firemen's Relief Association. (Two members of the LAFD centennial book review committee were Dick Baker and Jim Perry – previously mentioned).

Harry & Wally's Favorite TV Shows, 1989, by Walter Podrazik & Harry Castleman, Prentice Hall, Pub.

Playing Doctor: Television, Storytelling, and Medical Power, 1989, by Joseph Turow, Oxford University Press, NY.

London's Burning, 1989, by Jack Rosenthal, Robson Books Ltd. Publisher, Copyright LWT

Lights! Camera! Safety! 1991, revision 1998 by Michael McCann Ph.D., C.I.H. (A Health and Safety Manual for Motion Pictures and Television Production)

Unsold TV Pilots, The Almost Complete Guide to Everything You Never Saw on TV 1955-1990, by Lee Goldberg, 1991, Citadel Press Book, Carol Publishing Group.

Television Detective Shows of the 1970s, 1991, by David Martindale, McFarland & Co. Inc., Pub.

London's Burning - Behind the Scenes, 1992, by Geoff Tibballs, Boxtree Ltd., Pub.

The Radio Times Yearbook – 1993, edited by Alison Wear, published by Ravette Books

London's Burning - Behind the Blaze, 1995, by Geoff Tibballs,

Boxtree Ltd., Pub.

The Emergency! Companion, 1995, by Jim Page, Jems Communications

The Complete Directory To Prime Time Network TV Shows, 1946-Present, (3rd Edition, 1985) & (6th edition, 1995), by Tim Brooks and Earle Marsh, Ballantine Publishing Group.

On the Line, December 2001, Published by the Internal Communications Office of the LA County FireDepartment

Fire Department of New York – An Operational Reference. 4th Edition, January 2002, by James S. Griffiths

Report From Ground Zero, March 2002, by Dennis Smith, Viking Penguin publisher

Fire Lover, June 2002 by Joseph Wambaugh, HarperCollins Publisher, NY

The Internet Movie Database

TV Guide (several issues), *Entertainment Weekly, and other regional weekly TV* magazines as noted.

Author, Richard Yokley and 1954 Mack.

ABOUT THE AUTHOR

Richard joined the ranks of the Bonita-Sunnyside Fire Department (near San Diego California) in 1972, rising to the rank of Operations Chief. Richard retired in December 1999 after almost twenty-eight years of service. He is the author of *The History of Fire Protection in Sweetwater Valley*, (an unpublished document) a fifty-year history of the Bonita-Sunnyside Fire Department. He received Firehouse Magazines "Heroism & Community Service Award" in 1987, and was also awarded his fire department's only Exemplary Service Award. Richard continues to serve the County of San Diego by serving on the Emergency Medical Care Committee.

Richard is currently involved with animal rescue, and works at SeaWorld San Diego as an EMT-D. Richard received the SeaWorld Excellence Award in 2000.

If you have any additions or comments, he can be reached at P.O Box 718, Bonita, CA 91908. They would be well-received and appreciated.
Bio: http://www.defrance.org/gvine/yokley.htm